How to Fix Karate
(Volume Two)

A Karate training and workout book

Al Case

cover photo
Kanō Tsunenobu, Public domain, via Wikimedia Commons

Table of Contents

WORKS BY AL CASE

<u>MARTIAL ARTS BOOKS</u>
How to Create Kenpo 1-3
<u>Encyclopedia of Martial Arts 1-5</u>
  Pan Gai Noon Karate/Kung Fu (vol 1)
  Kang Duk Won Korean Karate (vol 2)
  Kwon Bup American Karate (vol 3)
  Outlaw Karate (vol 4)
  Buddha Crane Karate (vol 5)
How to be a Master Instructor
<u>Matrix Karate</u>
  Matrix Karate: Vol 1 ~ White Belt
  Matrix Karate: Vol 2 ~ Green Belt
  Matrix Karate: Vol 3 ~ Brown Belt
  Matrix Karate: Vol 4 ~ Black Belt
  Matrix Karate: Vol 5 ~ Master
Binary Matrixing
How to Matrix the Martial Arts
Matrixing Chi

<u>NEUTRONICS</u> (philosophy)
The Neutronics Viewpoint
Prologue
Neutronics
The 24 Principles
Outside the Tube

<u>MARTIAL ARTS VIDEO COURSES</u>
Matrix Karate
Matrix Kung Fu
Matrix Aikido
Master Instructor Course
Shaolin Butterfly
Butterfly Pa Kua Chang
Five Army Tai Chi Chuan
Chiang Nan
Matrixing Kenjutsu
Blinding Steel
Create Your Own Martial Art
Evolution of a Martial Art 1-3
  Pan Gai Noon
  Kang Duk Won
  Kwon Bup
Outlaw Karate
Temple Karate
The Black Belt Course
Rolling Fists

<u>NOVELS</u>
The North Mansion
The Haunting of House
Machina
<u>Monkeyland Series 1-6</u>
  Monkeyland
  The Bomber
  The Madman
  The Lone Star Revolt
  Yancy
  Return to Monkeyland
<u>Yancy Yelkins 1-3</u>
  Small in the Saddle
  When the Cold Wind Blows
  When the Black Dog Dies
<u>The Wizard of Parts 1-3</u>
  Path of the Snake
  Path of the Wizard
  Path of the Dragon
<u>The Hero and Assassin 1-3</u>
  Hero
  Assassin
  Avatar
Falling Skies
Pack
Twisted Gods
Lobo Love
How to Make a God

<u>YOGA</u>
Yogata: The Yoga Kata
Black Belt Yoga
Light of Insane Yogi's Eyeballs (shorts)

<u>CHILDREN'S BOOKS</u>
Universal Glue
Return of the Dragon

<u>MISCELLANEOUS</u>
The Truth About Algebra
Make Your Own Secret Language
Blood and Ink (How to Write)

AlCaseBooks.com
MonsterMartialArts.com
ChurchofMartialArts.com

SPECIAL NOTE

At the beginning of some chapters you will find links to videos showing the forms.

If these links do not work, then <u>retain your receipt</u> for the book(s) and email me for new links.

This is likely to happen as links can corrode over time, websites can be taken down, replaced, and so on.

Al Case at: Aganzul@gmail.com.

Have you read the first half of this book?

How to Fix Karate (Volume One)

Introduction

In 1967, almost 55 years ago at the time of this writing, I began Karate.

For near 55 years I have practiced, studied, sweated, explored, and had more fun than a barrel of monkeys having sexual relations with another barrel of monkeys.

For near 55 years I have written of my studies, writing book after book, detailing what I was learning.

I discovered Matrixing and Neutronics, developed arts, and taught thousands of people.

And thousands of people have taught me.

What a blast, eh?

55 years ago I was in a backyard, fantasizing. Beating hordes of imaginary opponents. Dreaming of being an honorable person.

This evening, and hopefully for many more evenings, I will be in my backyard, fantasizing. Beating hordes of imaginary opponents. Dreaming of being an honorable person.

Full circle.

The beginning is the end, and the end is the beginning.

For almost 55 years my books have described my life, my life in the arts. I have written and offered what I learned, tried to correct my impressions as I went, and had a great time.

If the day was dark, I could always run through my forms.
If I had bad emotions I could easily work them out.
When people came to me in less than a peaceful frame of mind…I could handle them.
And this is the essence of this art that I describe.
I wish this peace to all.

In a world gone insane, people need Karate and the peace and strength of the true martial arts.

As Gichin said, "The Way: who will pass it on straight and well?"

I hope it will be you.

Al Case

Chapter Twenty-Six
Pinan Four
(section one)

To win one hundred victories in one hundred battles is not the highest skill. To subdue the enemy with out fighting is the highest skill. ~ Gichin Funakoshi

Below are the bonus videos for Pinan Four.

pinan 4 front.mp4   https://youtu.be/xN8kKpVumBU

pinan 4 side   https://youtu.be/cpwoiX7_jnQ

pinan 4 explanation.mp4   https://youtu.be/c_WvtO3xKZg

Pinan Four
section one

As with Pinan Three, there is an amazing amount wrong with the first move of the form, and this simply because the 'masters' only included the first blocking move, and left out all attacks. In my vision of the form I have given you four potential attacks, with a *lot* of potential techniques hidden between the lines.

Begin from a natural stance. Feet shoulder width apart and square. Relaxed. Able to move in any direction without first leaning.

Pivot to the left and bring the hands up the center as if scooping. The hips should be square (facing forward).

Pivot the hips slightly to the right (to align with the feet and shoulders) as you execute a left knife hand block and a right high knife hand block. You can do these as blocks or grabs.

Bring the right hand down as if in a chop. You could chop the neck, but the reason for the open hand is to grab the neck. You can do this move with a front stance or a back stance.

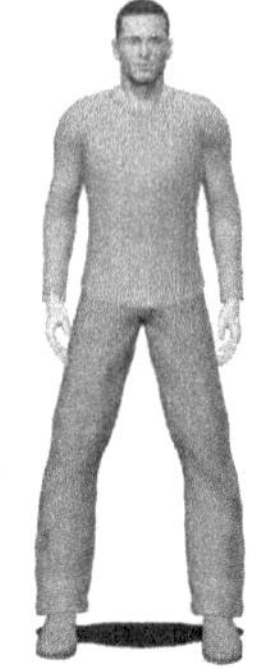

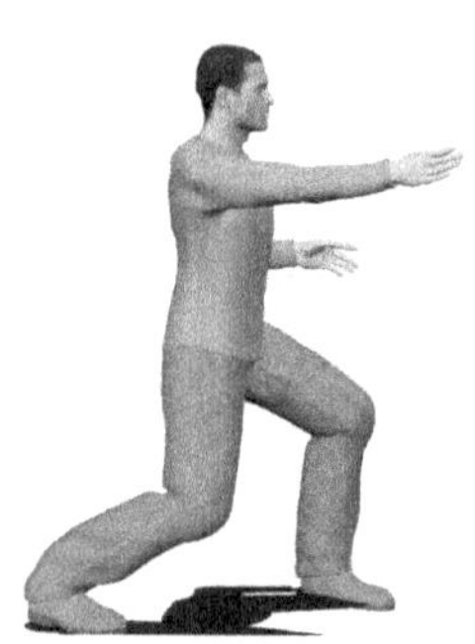

Pinan Four
Application One

This first move breaks the oral tradition of doing one thing at a time. If you wish to adhere to the concept of doing one thing at a time stagger the blocks, doing first one, then the other.

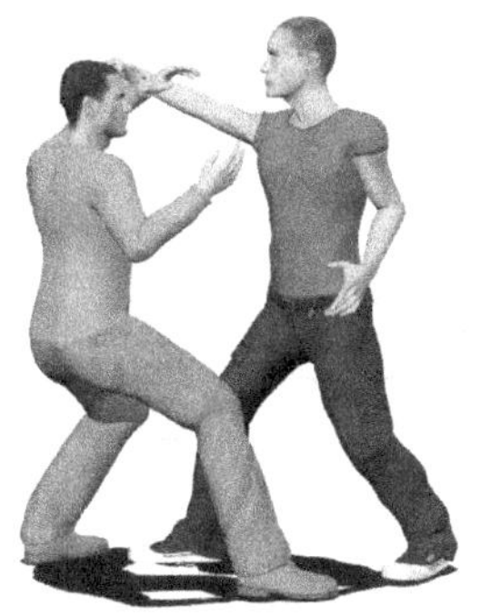

For instance, the attacker steps forward with the right foot and punches with the right hand. The defender steps back with the left foot into a back stance as he executes a left high block (grab). His right hand is there, but not doing anything.

The attacker then punches with the left hand. The defender executes a right knife hand to the attacker's left arm.

The defender then jams the thumb of his right hand into the side of the neck of the attacker.

He could also, on the initial chop to the arm, make a chop to the collar bone, breaking it.

Pull the right hand down and slap the right knee.

Return to the double knife hand blocking position.

Extend the left hand as if in a spear. Again, it can be a chop or spear, but it is meant to be a grab of the neck.

Pull the left hand down and slap the left knee.

Pinan Four
Application Two

The attacker steps forward with the right foot and punches with the right hand. The defender steps forward with the right foot and executes a left high block and a right knife hand.

The blocks aren't blocks, however, so much as grabs. The left hand grabs the attacker's right hand and pushes it up. The right hand grabs the shoulder and pulls down. At the same time the defender raises his knee into the groin or midsection of the attacker.

There are several places to go with this technique. One could simply throw the attacker on the ground, one could turn the attacker into a vertical arm pin, one could sweep him (usually before the downward pull, but…whatever), and so on.

One reason I stumbled on this as the defense was because the hands are open. In pinan two the hands are closed because the fist must hit. In pinan four the hands are open, which leads to grabs and grab arts.

One can also use a kick or a foot sweep.

Return to the double knife hand block position.

Execute a right elbow strike to the left palm. You can do this into a forward stance if you wish. You may also reach out with the left hand prior to executing the elbow strike.

Return to the double knife hand block position.

Extend the right hand as if chopping.

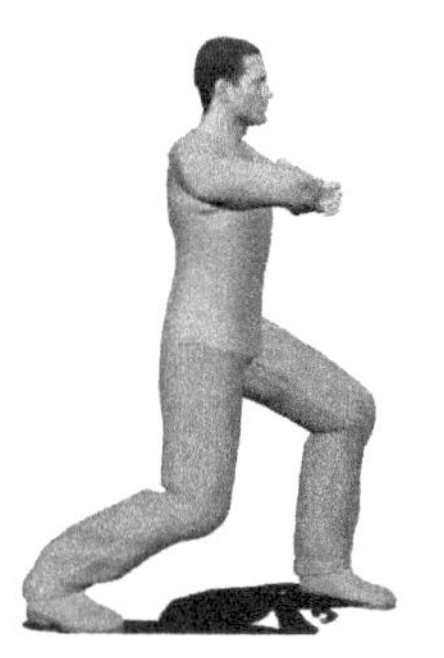

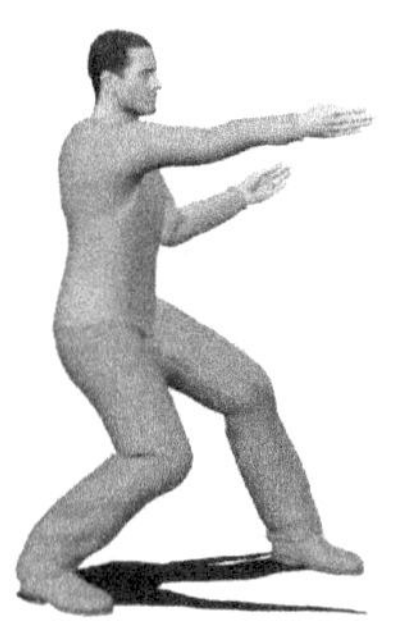

Pinan Four
Application Three

One can practice this application after blocking a right punch with a knife hand.

The defender steps forward with the left foot as he grabs the attacker by the back of the neck with the left hand and executes a right elbow strike to the face.

The defender pushes the right arm against the attacker's neck and raises the attacker's arm to spiral him into a vertical arm pin.

The original technique in the Kang Duk Won ended with the elbow strike, but because I believe the outward middle block was more designed for a grab than a block, it only makes sense to continue the technique with a throw that should definitely end the fight.

This throw is difficult for the sole reason that the student always wants to push the arms either in a vertical circle, or a horizontal circle. They must be pushed up at an angle between the vertical and the horizontal. This results in a diagonal spiral which is very effective. This is called the 'vertical' arm pin because it doesn't work well unless you take the opponent's arm, push it in a diagonal spiral, and make it vertical to the ground.

Execute a left elbow strike to the right palm.

Step/pivot into a horse stance as you execute a left chop and a right high knife block.

Pivot right 180 degrees, hips squared, and scoop the hands up the center line.

Turn the hips slightly to the left as you execute a right knife hand block and a left high knife hand block.

By this time in a student's progress he should be exploring other distances, such as for the elbows or knees.

The attacker steps forward with the right foot and strikes with the right hand. The defender executes a left high block hand.

The attacker strikes with the left hand. The defender executes a right knife hand.

The defender can shuffle forward executing a right vertical elbow strike to the face.

And/or grab the attacker's back of the neck with his right hand and move forward to execute a left horizontal elbow to the face.

There is also the possibility of pulling the attacker down into a knee strike with the rear leg.

You should explore the matrix of doing the opening move, then exploring: right knee, left knee, right elbow, left elbow, chop neck right, chop neck left, and so on.

Bring the left hand down as if chopping.

Pull the left hand down and slap the left knee with the palm.

Return to the double knife hand block position.

Extend the right arm as if chopping. I show the student extending his hand in a back stance. Some people will prefer the front stance. Either way is fine, and you would adapt the stance as necessary for distance when applying this move.

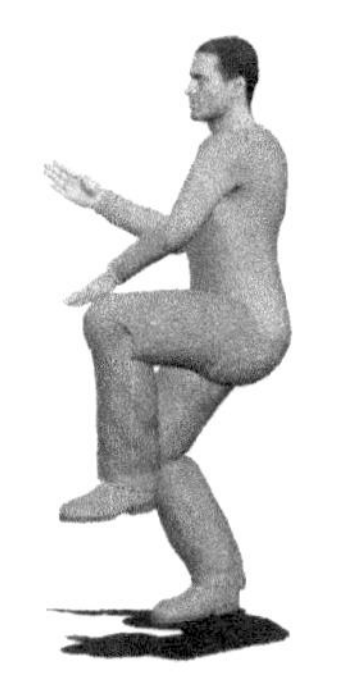

Why Not Question the Masters?

History tends to be a very white-washed affair.

Everybody bows down to the masters, considers them very special people with remarkable intelligence and insight. Amazing people who came to earth and blessed everyone with their intelligence, and never made a mistake.

The founder of an art called Pa Kua Chang was rumored to grab the tail of a horse and run for twenty miles.

Long after he died his daughter was asked whether there was any truth in that story. She grinned and said, "My father used to laugh at that story."

One of the more important people in Karate, Matsumura Sōkon, was rumored to have glared at a bull and cowed him. (Sorry about that pun. Not.) It turned out that before he fought the bull he went to his pen every night, waited until the bull came to sniff him. He then stabbed the bull in the nose with a large pin. No wonder the bull didn't want to mess with him!

The point here is that rumor and gossip build legends. And the real point is that these so called 'masters' lived their lives and everybody kow towed and nobody ever asked why what they were doing made no sense.

Look at the things I've mentioned so far. Pinan one being worthless. The opening sequences of Pinan Three and Pinan Four being nothing but incomplete techniques.

Why didn't anybody ever ask one of these so-called 'masters' why?

Instead, students take this worthless garbage and make it mystical, and never understand that the word 'mystical' means 'something that you don't know.' But all they had to do was look at the technique, and ask a few questions, and they would know.

Look, those old fellows that we call 'Masters,' sometimes they have to be respected. They lived through rough times and did what they did. And they did pass the art along.

But they were like you and I, they made mistakes, they screwed up, and you would better be served if you asked them why they screwed up rather than worshipping them like some sort of God.

Pull the right hand down and slap the knee.

Return to the double knife hand blocking position.

Pivot the hips to the square position as you execute a left elbow to the right palm.

Return to the double knife hand blocking position.

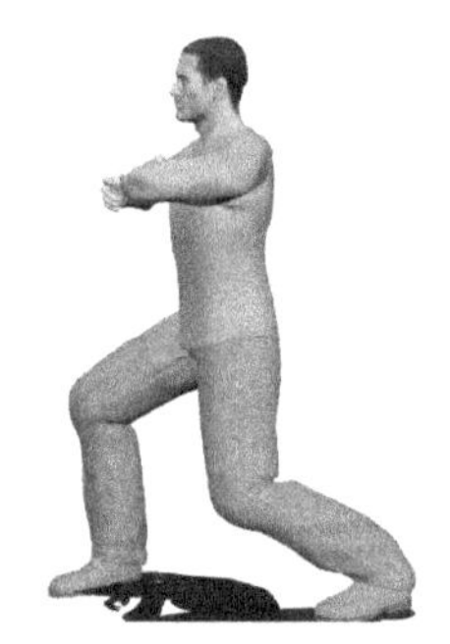

Why are Stances So Low?

Back in the thirties and forties Gichin had a son, Gigo. Gigo is credited with establishing much of the modern Shotokan base. He advocated high kicks, low stances, and helped work the forms so they reflected these concepts.

Now, we all know that low stances are the coolest looking things. To be low, like a snake, then leap through the air with dazzling power. Isn't that what karate is all about?

Well, maybe. But consider; the first karateka, way before Gigo and even Gichin, had higher stances. Why? Maybe they were lazy, maybe they had lower stances when they were young. Maybe they just found high stances were better for fighting.

A higher stance can be more mobile than a low stance, and therefore of more use.
Do you ground better when you are lower? Yes. But you can't move as fast as you would like. And you are more prone to certain types of attacks.

Now, this is not to say that low stances are bad, I actually believe in them. But to judge karate from the viewpoint that a low stance is the end all be all is foolish. You should be able to be low or high, depending on the need.

And, that said, I practice in a higher stance for an entirely different reason: being older, if I practice low stances I can only work out for a certain amount of time, then I am tired, my legs are tired, and that's the end of my work out.

But if I have a higher stance I can work out all day long without becoming too tired, or too weak in the legs.

So, high or low, it's up to you, but consider what I have said here before you decide there is only one right way to do Karate.

Bring the left hand down as if chopping. Front stance optional.

Execute a right elbow strike to the left palm.

Step/pivot into a horse stance as you execute a right chop and a left high knife hand bock.

Bring the left foot up to the right and roll the right hand over so that the right one is pointing up to the side, and the left one is covering the body.

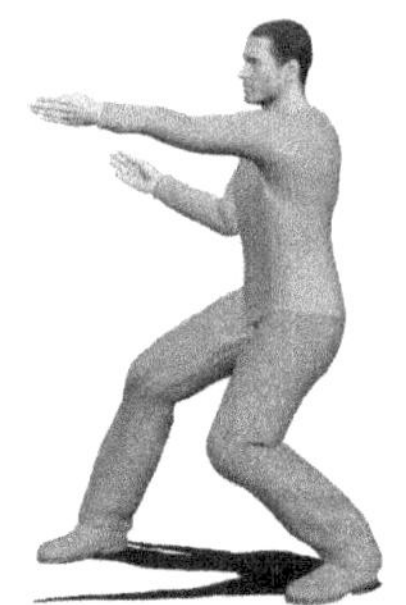

Chapter Twenty-Seven
Pinan Four
(section two)

Many Karate teachers teach a watered down style — no hip action and no depth of punching — so it is easy to say that these teachers have no depth to their knowledge. You are what your teacher is, and if he knows a lot, you should be able to demonstrate this knowledge. ~ Yuchoku Higa

Pinan Four
Section Two

This is another example of how I have put circles back into the form. In the classical form you would simply step from figure one to figure four. But with the circles you can see the hands creating several potential blocks.

With the circles the student steps forward with the left foot into a front stance as he executes a cross wrist low block,

The student pulls the left foot back as he moves the right hand up and the left hand down in circles.

The student is in an hourglass stance as he executes an inverted pole position. The left hand protecting the face with a palm and the right hand protecting the midsection with in inverted forearm.

The student steps forward with the right foot into a front stance, simultaneously blocking with the right outward middle block.

Pinan Four
Application Four

The attacker kicks with the right foot. The defender charges forward, jamming the attacker and stopping the foot before it reaches full power. (Full extension = full power).

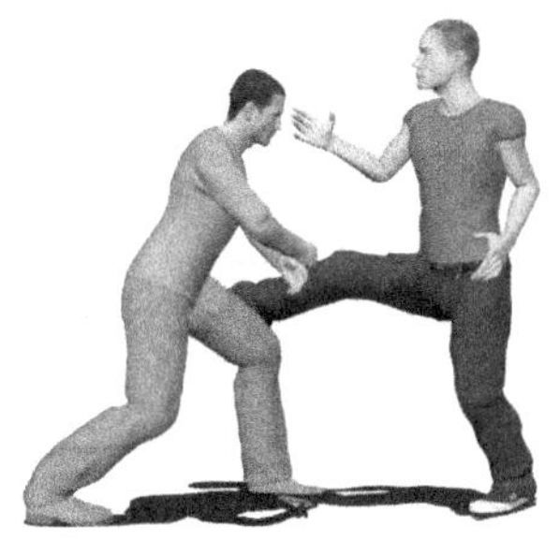

The defender then steps forward with the right foot and executes a right uppercut to the chin with the full weight of his body behind it.

If the attacker has armor on he will still be thrust away, but there is a chance the fist could strike the throat, ending the attack right then and there.

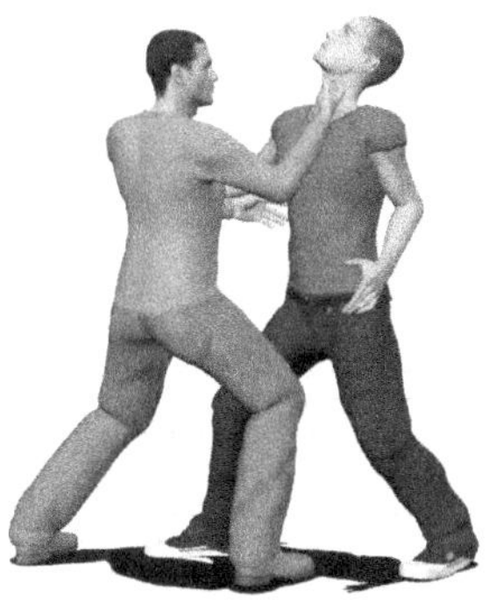

One has to step forward with the correct foot, and have the correct hand on top, in the initial move.

If one steps forward with the wrong foot, or the distance requires it, the alternative would be to shuffle forward so as to execute the strike, as in figure three.

In the crossed wrist low block the arms should be turned so that a single bone in the forearm is not presented. While accomplished karateka wouldn't be bothered by this, and might even break the attacker's leg, beginners should turn the arms so that each arm presents two bones. This dissipates the energy so they aren't harmed by the extra mass of the leg. Later, when they have figured out how to create their own sense of time in a technique, their own universe, they can go to the single bone blocks and break attacker's legs.

I do, however, believe the crossed low block move is more for grabbing than breaking. You will see that in the next technique.

I use circles to expand applications and make them more understandable.

From the last move of the last sequence the student is in a front stance with an augmented middle outward block.

The student raises his left hand and begins circling the arm. (Figure 2)

The student continues circling to the left inverted low block and a right palm block as he brings the left foot upward and turned to the left.

The original form had a cat stance at this point, I prefer to keep both feet flat on the ground for better grounding. The front foot is drawn back slightly.

The student executes a simultaneous left outward block and a right parry and a left front kick. Open hand, fist or grab is optional.

Some systems have this as a side kick. The original masters of karate didn't seem to put a lot of emphasis on the side kick, and especially a high one, so I prefer to stay with the front snap kick that I originally learned.

Also, a side kick requires too much hip turn for the following elbow strike.

Pinan Four
Application Five

This variation on the cross low block is more complex, but still works well as an arm take down.

The attacker steps forward with the right foot and executes a right punch. The defender charges forward to jam the technique and applies the cross block to the arm.

The defender reaches over the elbow and finds the bone under the elbow. He pulls up on the elbow at the same time as he pushes down on the wrist. The result is an armlock (elbow roll) that can move into a vertical arm pin.

The attacker must have the correct arm on top or the technique will fail and fall to striking techniques.

The real joy here is that the defender, once he has figured out the lock, can immediately apply it to a knife disarm. Simply give the attacker a knife and let the defender figure out how to apply the technique without getting cut.

In spite of all cautions, one of the senior instructors at the Kang Duk Won practiced with a real knife. Man, you should have seen the blood.

The student sets forward into a front stance while executing a right elbow strike to the left palm.

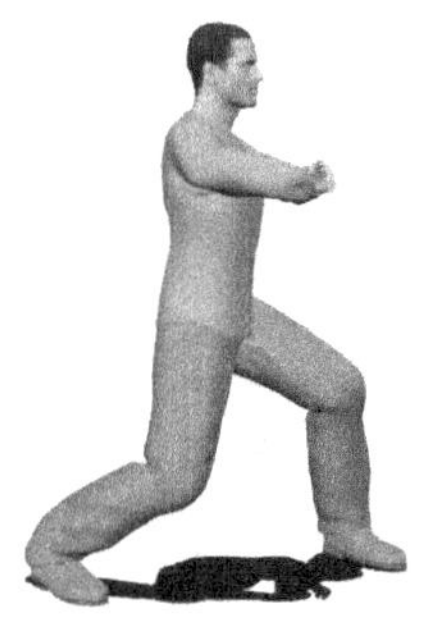

The student pivots 180 degrees, swinging his right arm through a low block and raising his right hand through a high block.

The right leg is pulled back and the student executes the left palm block and a right inverted low block. He is obviously duplicating the move he has just done on the opposite side.

This is an interesting application in that one is doing three things at once. This goes against a specific oral teaching which advises that one must do only one thing at a time.

As with everything, oral teachings can be taken with a grain of salt.

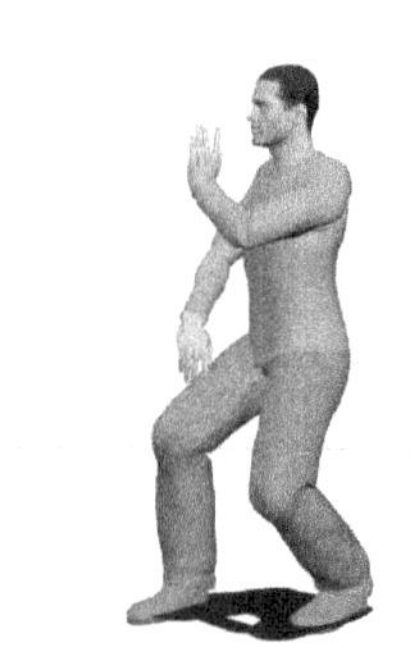

If one did only one thing at a time there would only be one or two techniques in this move, starting from a simple palm block or parry.

But one could apply this to a two hand push or grab and find simple but useful techniques using two hands.

I've always felt that simple grabs should be learned, then blocks for single punches, then combinations for multiple punches, then adding throws, and, finally, applying the throw without going through the blocks…just grabbing a hand or foot out of the air and throwing.

Pinan Four
Application Six

One could simply X block down (figure 1) and move into the middle block of figure four, which was probably the original technique. Introducing the circles, however, allows us to expand the basic move into a sequence of blocks resulting multiple techniques and the 'body bumping' of figure four.

The attacker executes a right kick, the defender executes a left foot forward X low block. (figure 1)

The attacker strikes with the left hand, the defender executes a right high block.

The attacker strikes with the right hand, the defender executes a left palm block.

The defender moves in with the right foot and executes a right outward middle block to create a 'splitting technique.'

Examine the technique closely, change the sequence of blocks and strikes, and you will find many more techniques inside this simple move.

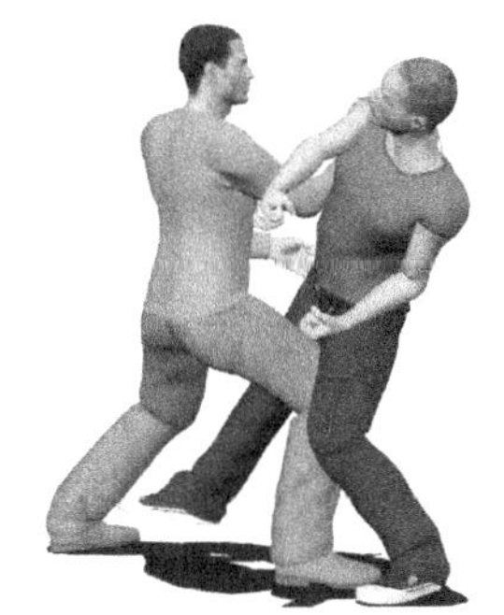

From the last move (the kick), step forward and execute a left horizontal elbow to the right palm.

Turn the head to the left as you execute a right high block and a left low block.

Pivot to the front as you execute a left high block and a right chop (as if to the neck).

We used to practice a basic hip twist exercise at the beginning of every class. The stance pivots and the hips slam into place. It was one of those slow but steady power builders that helped the student create internal energy.

Execute a right front snap kick as you guard the face with a right palm and protect the belly with a left dangling forearm. The left dangling forearm would be a parry.

Pinan Four
Application Seven

The attacker kicks with the right leg. The defender steps to the right side into a front stance facing to the right as he simultaneous executes a left low block and a right high block.

The defender pivots to the front (left) into a front stance as he executes a left high block and a right chop to the neck. Definitely a fight ender.

It was common practice to break bricks in the Kang Duk Won. We chopped 'em, we punched 'em, we broke them seven ways from go.

One of the tricks was to hold one brick over another brick and drop the brick just as you hit it. This gave a sharper focus to the brick being struck, and it would then separate easily.

Once you got good at the trick you simply hit the brick and it broke.

Throughout Karate there are stories of people who broke stones with their bare hands. Who twisted bundles of bamboo shoots until the they broke. These stories are real. Unfortunately, students today are more interested in getting a belt, or fighting in a tournament, and they don't take the time to cultivate the real power needed to perform these tricks.

And, please, don't fall for the old Bruce Lee saying, 'Boards don't fight back.'

The reason we broke boards was to sharpen our technique, to be able to use the power of the break in our techniques.

It worked.

Stomp the right foot down as you bring the left foot up behind it in a cross stance. At the same time you stomp you should be executing a right backfist.

This is a classic example of stomping the foot to increase the weight which requires (causes) more energy. I call this supercharging.'

As this is an unbalanced stance. I prefer to put it together with a throw, or evasion move.

Pinan Four
Application Eight

There are a lot of ways to do this technique. This is the way we did it in the Kang Duk Won.

The attacker steps forward with the right foot sand punches with the right hand. The defender executes a right inward block and a right kick to the body.

The defender retracts the foot and grabs the attacker's right arm with his left hand.

The defender pulls the attacker forward and stomps the right foot, supercharging a backfist to the face of the attacker.

I added the throw later, it seemed that the KDW technique was only a half a technique, especially as the stomping position will be momentarily weak and unbalanced after the expression of extra power. The defender extends the right arm on the left side of the attacker's neck and pushes up and around (diagonally) on the attacker's right arm with his left hand. This results in a vertical arm pin.

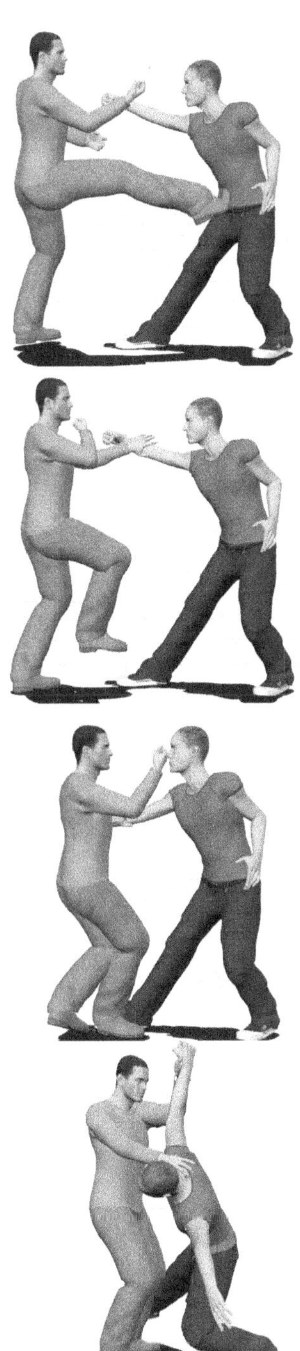

Pinan Four
Application Nine

The attacker steps forward with the right foot and punches with the right hand. The defender executes a left high block.

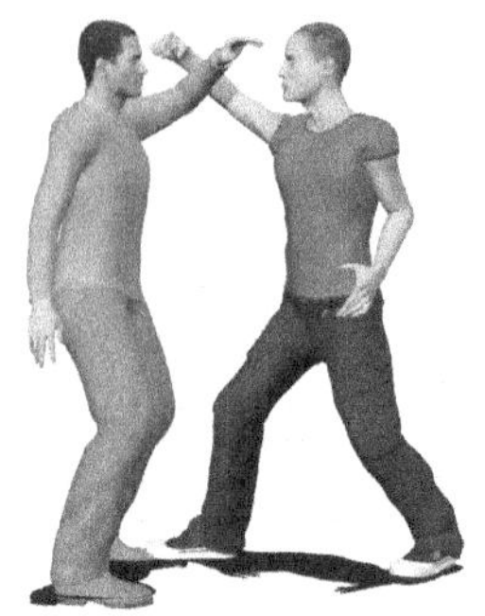

The attacker punches to the body with the left hand. The defender executes a right parry.

The defender executes a left outward middle block and a left front kick.

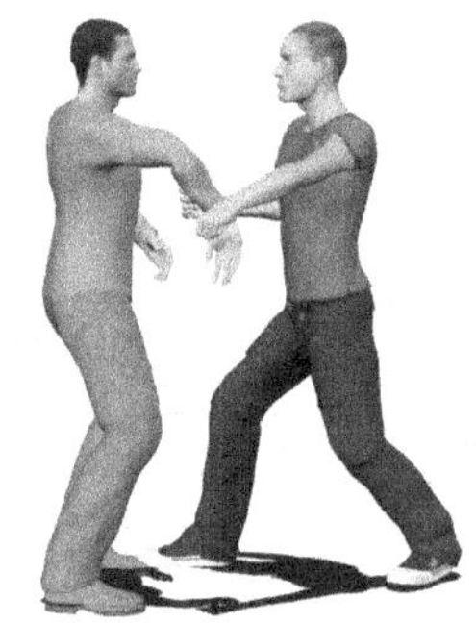

The defender sets forward with the left foot into a front stance as he hooks the attacker's neck with the left hand and pulls his face into a right horizontal elbow strike.

One can easily push the right arm up (diagonally) and the head down to affect a throw, as is shown in previous techniques.

Chapter Twenty-Eight
Pinan Four
(section three)

To all those whose progress remains hampered by ego-related distractions, let humility – the spiritual cornerstone upon which Karate rests – serve to remind one to place virtue before vice, values before vanity and principles before personalities. ~ Sokon 'Bushi' Matsumura

Pinan Four
section three

From the stomp pivot 225 degrees to the left, this is 45 degrees past 180 degrees, into a back stance. Bring the hands up the center in a scooping motion.

Bring the hands down and outward in double outward grabbing block. The hips should be square.

Execute a right front snap kick with a right cross palm block.

Set forward with the right foot into a front stance as you execute a left punch.

Execute a right punch.

The punches have to be in this sequence because if you strike somebody with a lunging punch they will then be out of range of the reverse punch. Reverse punch first and the opponent may still be within range of the lunging punch.

Pinan Four
Application Ten

The attacker steps forward with the left foot and pushes to the chest with both hands.

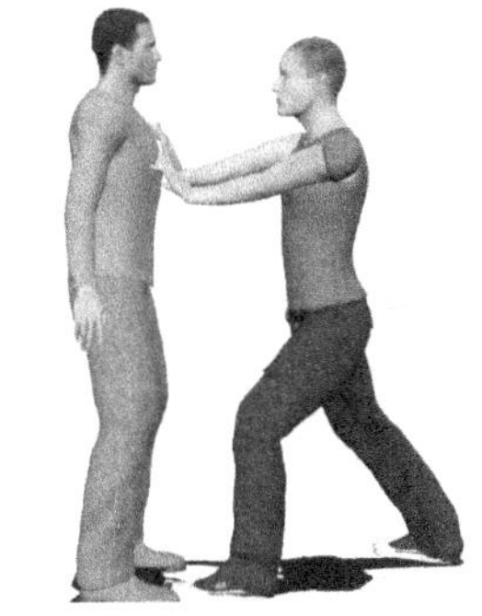

The defender steps back with the right foot into a back stance as he executes two outward middle blocks. The blocks are grabs.

The defender pulls the attacker forward and off balance as he executes a left kick to the mid-section.

The defender sets forward as he punches to the chest with the right hand. Obviously, he can execute a second punch as is shown in the form.

As the student gets better and better he will find that his kick speeds up and matches the hand speed of the attacker easily. Eventually he will be grabbing and kicking in one smooth motion, the parts of the technique will become quite harmonious.

Bring the right foot back and extend it 90 degrees to the right (45 degrees past the centerline of the form). Bring the hands inward and up in a scooping motion.

Bring the hands down and outward in outward grabbing blocks. The hips should be squared.

Execute a left snapping kick as you protect the face with the left cross palm block.

Set forward with the left foot into a front stance as you execute a right punch.

Execute a left punch.

You should make the kick a momentarily lock. Thus you are practicing both the snap kick and the thrust kick.

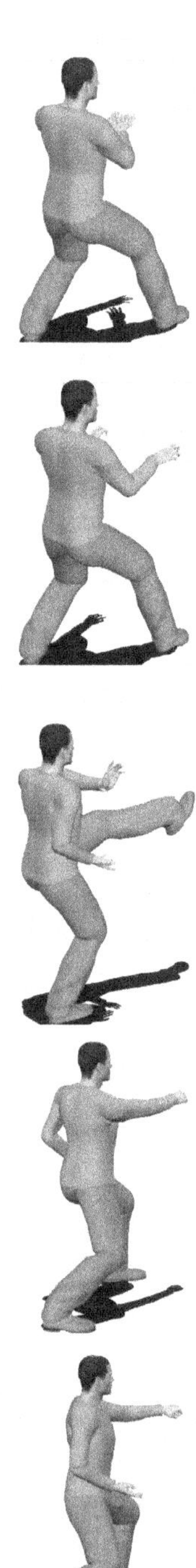

Pinan Four
Application Eleven

The attacker steps forward with the right foot and punches with the right hand. The defender executes a right front snap kick to the groin as he executes a right cross palm block.

The student reaches over the attacker's fist and grips the hand. He pivots slightly to the right as he turns the hand into a wrist lock.

Obviously, this defense could be used for a punch with either hand.

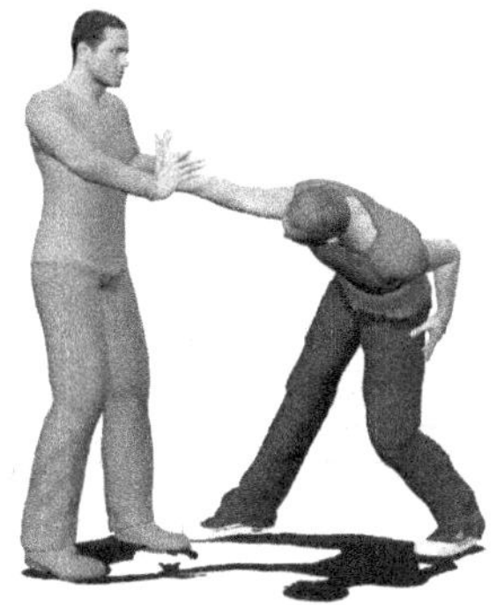

I often show this technique for a grab to the throat before I have the student grab a punch out of the air. It's easier to learn that way.

Enough practice and you can apply this in freestyle. If the fellow doesn't go with it, or if you decide force is better than flow, simply supercharge a stomp and chop the attacker's neck.

Just to differentiate, when I say throat I usually mean the front of the neck. When I say neck I refer to the side of the neck.

Bring the left leg back as you slap downward and inward with the left hand.

Continue the motion of the left hand as you extend the left leg into a back stance and execute a left outward block. (Can be an uppercut.)

Retract the left foot as you protect the face with a left palm block and the body with a right dangling forearm block.

Continue the motion of the arms and circle the right up through a high block and the left hand down through a low block.

The stance while circling the arms is an hourglass.

This sequence, including the moves on the next page, can be looped in different ways! It is helpful to focus on pushing from one leg to the other.

Pinan Four
Application Twelve

Here is the application using the circles I re-introduced to the form.

The attacker steps forward with the right foot and punches with the right hand. The defender steps back with the right foot into a back stance as he executes a left cross palm block.

The attacker executes a left punch. The defender executes a right high block.

The attacker punches with the left hand. The defender executes a left cross palm as he steps forward with the right foot.

The defender assumes a right back stance as he smothers (parries outward?) the attackers right and executes a right uppercut to the throat.

Modern karate has tons of forms, but how many does a person need? Past calisthenics, there aren't really any more significant techniques, because there are no advanced techniques, there are only better basics.

Circling the hands, however, and blocking series of strikes enables the student to better 'enter the moment' and achieve the state of 'mushin no shin,' or 'mind of no mind.' Mushin no shin is to enter 'now' without mental distractions.

Continue the circling of the arms (clockwise) through the left palm block and the left dangling forearm.

Step forward with the right foot into a back stance as you execute a right outward grabbing block.

Retract the right foot as you executes a right palm block and a left dangling forearm block.

Continue the circling of the hands (counter clockwise) through a left high block and a right low block.

I call this the 'six blocks.' If you examine this circling of the hands you will find six separate blocks inside that 'windmill.' This allows for a tremendous variety of combinations.

The Matrix of Throws

There are eight 'joints' specific to throwing.:
wrist twist in/wrist twist out
elbow roll/arm bar/inversion
shoulder roll forward/shoulder roll back
neck crank to right/neck crank to left
splitting
hip throw
knee take downs
ankle twists/sweeps

Whether you go right or left, in or out, or whatever, will depend on your position, whether you are inside the attack or outside, and so on.

You should be able to go back and forth from one lock to another without hesitation or error, or at least know which throws do not go back and forth easily. Below is a matrix giving 64 possible lock shifts. Practice them to find out which ones work and which don't.

	wrist	elbow	shoulder	neck	lower back	hip	knee	ankle
wrist								
elbow								
shoulder								
neck								
lower back								
hip								
knee								
ankle								

Continue the circling of the arms through a right palm block and a left dangling elbow.

Step forward with the left foot into a back stance as you execute a left outward grabbing block.

Step/shift the weight forward into a front stance as you execute double spear hands.

Pull the hands down and slap the right knee.

The bottom figure is a sideways viewpoint of the knee strike.

Pinan Four
Application Thirteen

The attacker steps forward with the right foot and punches with the right hand. The defender steps back with the right foot into a back stance and executes a right outward middle block.

The attacker executes a left strike. The defender shifts/steps forward and shoots his arms forward. He overrides the attacker's arm and pokes the attacker's eyes (or jabs the throat or breaks the collar bones or whatever).

The defender grabs the attacker's head and pulls him into a right knee strike.

While one could apply a throw at this point, the fact that the form calls for a foot stomp and pivot seems to be that the bodyguards were likely intent on rendering the attacker maimed or dead, and were spinning for the next attacker. Thus, explore for other techniques, especially grab arts, but consider what I have said here, and make your strike a killing one.

Twist the body to face in the other direction, 180 degrees, and stomp the right foot in a back stance as you execute a left knife hand block. This is pure 'supercharging.'

Stomp after the twist; do not stomp while you are twisting. It is a bad idea to increase weight on a joint in motion.

Retract the left foot as you begin triangle stepping. Protect the face with the left palm and scoop the right hand under. Make sure you are side stepping off the line of attack when triangle stepping.

Extend the right foot in a back stance as you execute a right knife hand block.

Return to the beginning stance of the form.

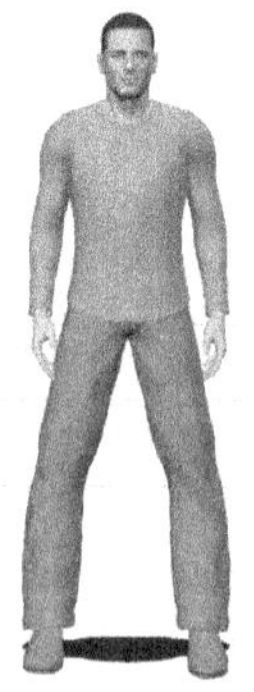

Chapter Twenty-Nine
Pinan Five
(section one)

Whatever luck I had, I made. I was never a natural athlete, but I paid my dues in sweat and concentration and took the time necessary to learn Karate and become World Champion. ~ Chuck Norris

Below are the bonus videos for Pinan Five.

pinan 5 front.mp4   https://youtu.be/RnljYb7qxtY

pinan 5 side   https://youtu.be/2j6Z322I7B0

pinan 5 explanation.mp4   https://youtu.be/F4vEpiOi96c

Pinan Five
section one

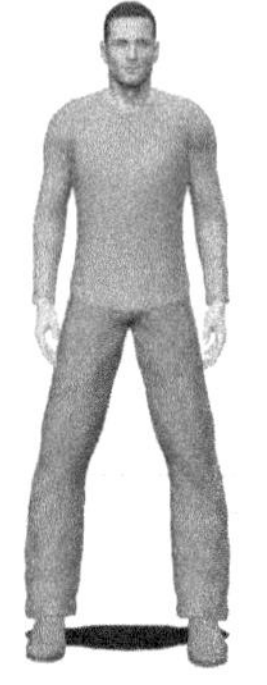

By this time a student should have become quite adequate at blocking and at grabbing. So the application for this technique will be slightly different.

From the ready position take a small step forward with the right foot and pivots to the left into a back stance. Simultaneously he executes a right cross palm bock. Notice how square the hips are. This will strengthen the circle of the blocking arm. Notice the left arm is in a scooping position.

Classically, one would execute an outward middle block, but the student should be fast enough now to start grabbing punches out of the air.

In the third image the student pivots his hips to the right to align them with the feet as he executes a left outward grabbing block.

The student executes a right punch from the back stance.

This move mimics the first move from pinan 3, and has the same counter and punch potentials.

Pinan Five
Application One

The attacker steps forward with the left foot and punches with the left hand. The defender steps back with the right foot into a back stance and executes a right cross palm block. The left hand is a 'scooping' position for the grab, or in the dangling forearm position for a block.

The attacker punches with the right hand. The defender can block, but matching the speed of the attacker's arm with his left hand and guiding/pulling him in is a superior technique. Note the hips turned to the right.

The defender pulls the attacker into his right punch. Note the hips turned back to the 'square' position.

This technique requires more speed than going out to block or simply grab, it requires the student to reach out and match the speed of the incoming punch.

Thus, the matrixed sequence of motion would be for the lower belts to block...the middle belts to grab...and the advanced belts to guide.

Some people think reaching out and guiding a strike is difficult. It is, but practice with single minded intention and dedication and fanaticism and it can be achieved. People who can't do it either don't really understand what is being asked for, and/or haven't practiced it enough.

Step to the right with the left foot and pivot 180 degrees into a back stance as you execute a right low block and a left high block. This is a transition position and not done with focus.

Continuing the motion of the arms the left hand executes a cross palm block. Hips are squared. This tends to 'coil' the hips for the next move.

Pivot the hips slightly to the left to align with the feet as you execute a left outward grabbing block.

Execute a left punch.

The palm blocks are useful, and the circling of the hands holds several blocks within them. You should explore this move and play with the various blocks and potential applications.

Pinan Five
Application Two

This is a variation of an earlier splitting technique. It can be done on either side, but takes a bit of work on one of the sides. In reality, it is a rude sort of 'body bump.'

The attacker steps forward with the right foot and punches with the right hand. The defender sinks into his hourglass stance and executes a left cross body palm block. He pivots very slightly to the right.

The attacker punches with the left hand. The defender executes a right cross body palm block. Again, a very slight pivot to the left.

The defender steps forward on the outside of the attacker's right foot with his left foot. He executes a left outward middle block. I would recommend you make the block more like a shoot, or a type of uppercut. You want to drive your weight into the the space of the opponent and send him flying.

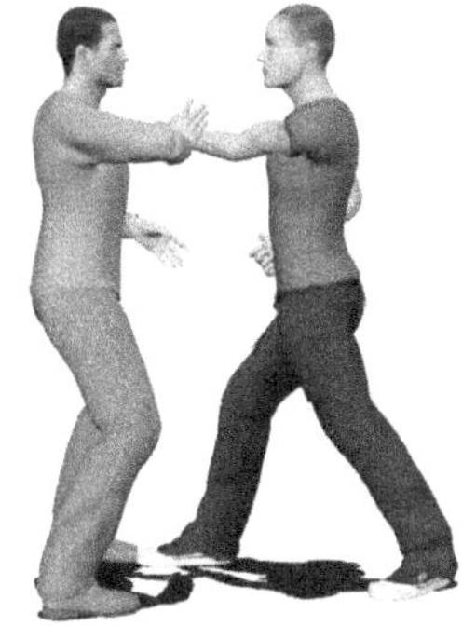

Hip Movement and Grounding

I have seen many martial artists overlook the movement of the hips in karate, and in other arts. The hips are the cornerstone of the body, they contain major weight, and when you strike or block you want to line up this weight into the attack or defense.

There is an exercise where you hold a broom stick across your hips and pivoted from front stance to front stance. You could tell how good your technique was by how the end of the broom stick focused, and whether it wiggled upon stopping.

Once, during my foolish youth, I actually hit somebody, and in that moment all my understanding of karate changed. When I impacted upon the fellow's chest I felt tremendous weight.

So a punch is…lifting a weight. Moving a weight.

All the air punches are fine, bag work is good, but the applications, when you actually learn to execute a controlled strike to a partner and move his weight…that is the gold.

A punch is measured by weight delivered.

Chapter Thirty
Pinan Five
(section two)

Karate cannot be adequately learned in a short space of time. Like a torpid bull, regardless of how slowly it moves, it will eventually cover a thousand miles. So too, for one who resolves to study Karate diligently two or three hours every day. After three or four years of unremitting effort one's body will undergo a great transformation revealing the very essence of Karate. ~ Anko Itosu

Pinan Five
section two

Step to the left with the right foot and pivot into a horse stance facing up the centerline of the form. Execute a left palm block.

Execute a left palm block.

At this point I hold my horse stance and go through the four circles I discussed in chapter three in the first book. I sometimes do this for quite a while, working on my meditation and the power of my horse.

The third figure is moving the right arm counter clockwise and the left arm clockwise, circling the arms inward.

The fourth figure is moving the right arm counterclockwise and the left arm clockwise., circling the arms outward.

Don't ignore the potential of the lower arm as a block or guide.

Pinan Five
Application Three

This technique is a 'what if' technique. I don't usually get into 'what if' techniques because all possible 'what ifs' are taken care of by simple matrixing. But this one, because it lends itself to specific counters, should be addressed.

The attacker kicks with the right foot. The defender moves forward and jams the attacker while executing a low crossed wrist block.

BUT…the defender blocked with the wrong hand on top of the crossed wrists and won't be able to affect a throw. Thus, because the defender has leaned his head into the defense the attacker will attack with a punch.

The defender, however, because he has seen the mistake he made, predicts this counter. He shifts back to a back stance and executes a left outward block (or a grab).

The defender grasps the attacker's right wrist and pulls him into a punch.

This technique should be matrixed, which is to say the student should be able to work the defense no matter which hand the attacker punches with, and he should explore both sides of the inward and outward blocks.

The student should also explore the technique with different legs being forward.

The top figure is moving the right arm counterclockwise and the left arm counterclockwise. This is a right slap and a left grab.

The second figure is moving the right hand clockwise and the left hand clockwise. This is a left slap and a right grab.

The third figure continues the right hand in a circle up to the open hand outward middle block position as he steps into a front stance with the right foot.

Retract the right leg (switch step) as as you circle the right hand down through the low block position.

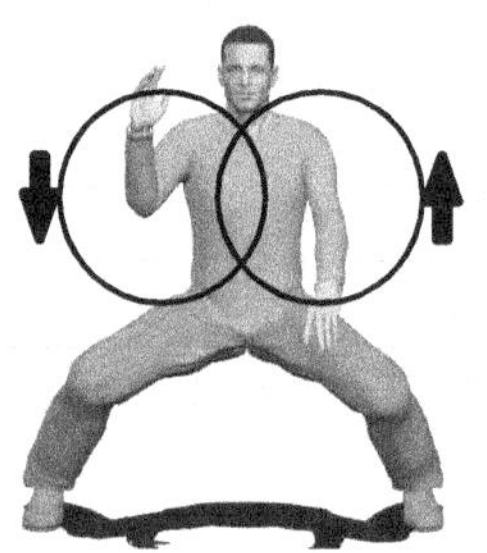

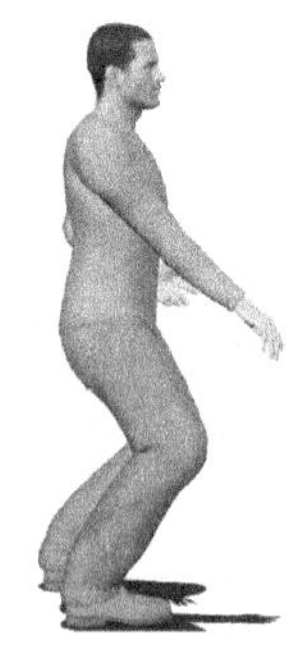

Pinan Five
Application Four

This technique looks weird, but it is actually the same as the arm twist from an earlier technique in Pinan Four. The only difference is that you are cranking the foot instead of the arm.

The attacker kicks with the right foot. The defender jams the kick with a cross wrist low block.

The defender reaches over grabs the attacker's heel with one hand, and presses down on the attacker's foot with the forearm.

This cranks the foot, turning the attacker over, and allowing the defender to wrap his arm over the leg, and to point at the ground.

Note that in the cross block the defender is turning his arms so the kick impacts on two of the bones in the forearms. This dissipates force, so that the larger bones don't break the smaller bones.

Also, while this block is referred to as a block, it is not a block. The purpose of a block is to cut the line of attack. The purpose of the crossed wrist low 'block' is to catch the kick.

One can adapt this to different kicks, even to the expanded technique of stepping in and tripping.

Continue the circle of the right hand through a palm block.

Step forward with the left foot into a front stance as you execute a crossed wrist low block.

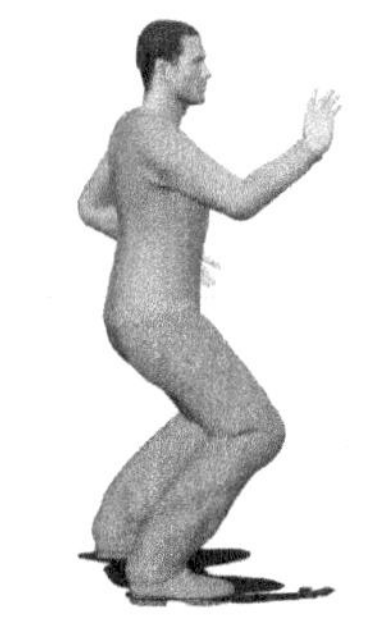

Shift back into a back stance as you execute a crossed wrist high block.

Fold the hands down as you start turning the hips to the right to align the hips and the feet.

This move is similar to a move in pinan three. The real difference is going to be in the applications. The student should have progressed to the point where he can pluck fists out of the air. He has worked the grab art of twisting the arm in Pinan Four, and now he is ready to start twisting the foot.

I call this technique 'Sword Catcher.' I changed it from the classical 'twine and horizontal back fist.' It is used to deal with a sword attack, but is now adapted for fisticuffs.

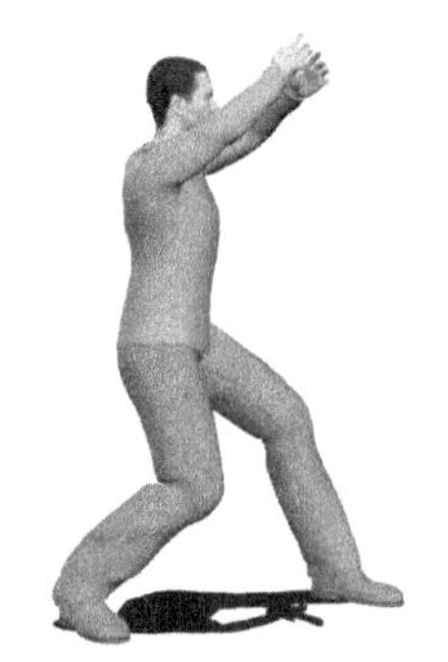

This technique provides an incredible amount of training in dealing with weapons, and really aids the intuitive process.

From the high crossed wrist block lower the hands and start to circle the left hand for an outward block.

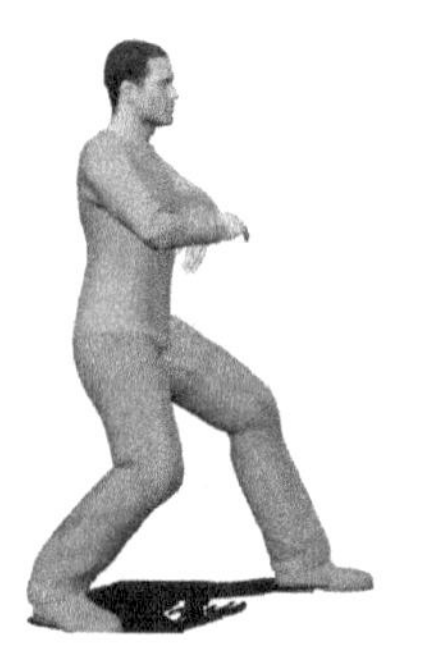

Pinan Five
Application Five

The attacker steps forward with the right foot and strikes directly down on the defender's head with a right chop. The defender steps forward and jams the attacker with a crossed wrist high block.

The defender pulls the attacker's wrist down with his right hand and pushes up on the attacker's elbow with his left forearm. This 'rolls' the attacker's arm.

If the attacker keeps a straight arm the defender takes technique in an arm bar. If the attacker bends his arm the defender takes him into an elbow roll.

The defender should pull the arm around so it is as if he is stepping into the attacker's arm pit.

As soon as the defender has this technique figured out it should be adapted to a knife or sword.

The defender should get to the point where he is not stopping the attack, but moving in front of it and absorbing it with no impact.

Continue the circle of the arms and roll the left hand over in a back fist/outward middle block.

Bring the left hand down in a reverse low (guiding) block.

Retract the left foot (switch step) as you circle the left hand through a claw (or a palm or whatever).

Step forward with the right foot into a front stance as you execute a right lunging punch.

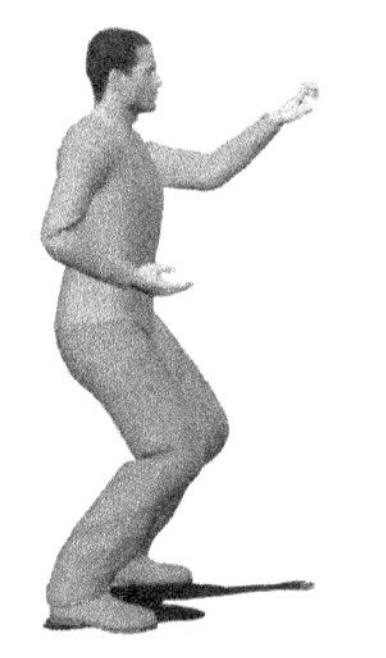

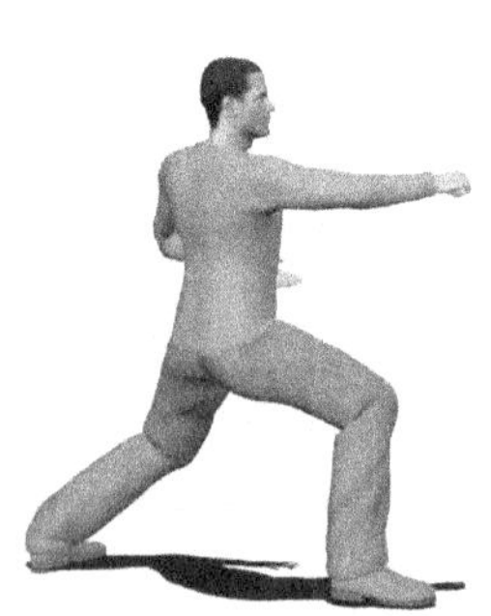

Pinan Five
Application Six

If the defender has the wrong leg forward, or the wrong arm on top, as pictured in the first image, he will set himself up for a counter. A left punch will be obvious and predictable.

As the attacker punches with the left arm, the defender shifts back, pivots slightly to the left to align the hips with the feet, and executes a right outward block to the attacker's left arm. Remember, the block should come down with gravity/weight!

The defender then grabs the attacker's left wrist with his right hand and pulls him into a left punch.

This technique should also be practiced with a knife, a sword, twisting the first attack over the punch, and so on.

This technique, as the last one, should be practiced with different arms, different legs forward, etc. The defender must become intuitive by exploring all the options, all the potentials of attack.

A nice option is to knuckle the biceps. Or to dig the fingers in in muscles (muscle separation technique). Or, if you're feeling really nasty, to chop the collar bone. A broken collar bone ends a fight real quick.

Pinan Five
Application Seven

Here's a little gift I discovered after some years of practice. I believe it may be practiced in Silat.

The attacker strikes down with the right chop. The defender catches the attack with the cross wrist high block.

The defender chops down on the attacker's neck, then pulls on the head while he pushes the arm up and around.

The result is a twist as if you are screwing the attacker right into the ground.

This one is a little weird, especially if you don't do it exactly right. If he resists you need practice. Or, you can just start slamming him in the face with elbows.

Chapter Thirty-One
Pinan Five
(section three)

The ultimate aim of Karate lies not in victory nor defeat, but in the perfection of the character of its participants. ~ Gichin Funakoshi

Pinan Five
section three

From the last position, swing the right arm and the right foot to the left 180 degrees as you bring the knee and the right hand up. I call it a sweeping block because the right forearm and right shin create a line which sweeps around the body.

Set down in a horse stance as you execute a right low block.

Swing the right arm across the body and execute a straight arm palm block to the left.

Retract the right arm as you execute a left punch. I call this a horse punch, or a Power Punch.

The power of this technique comes from the horse stance. The power of the horse stance comes from sinking the weight.

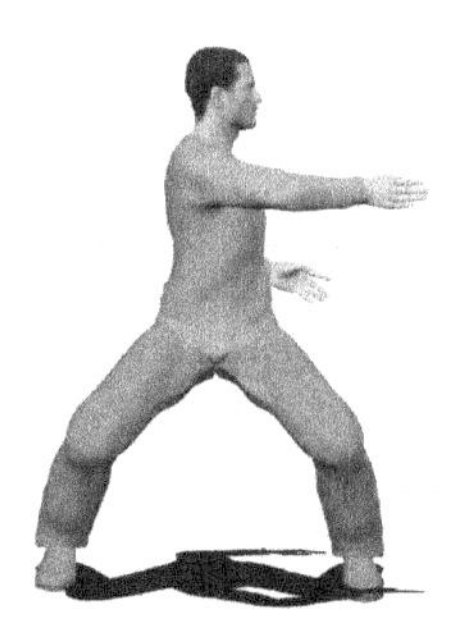

Students always make the mistake of thinking the horse stance, and other stances, are all about building strength. They are really about connecting energy to the earth.

It doesn't matter how high or low, how wide or narrow. What matters is that the student actually connects the energy of the body to the ground. This is done through hard training and focused mental abilities.

Pinan Five
Application Eight

The attacker steps forward with the left foot and punches with the left hand. The defender executes a sweeping block.

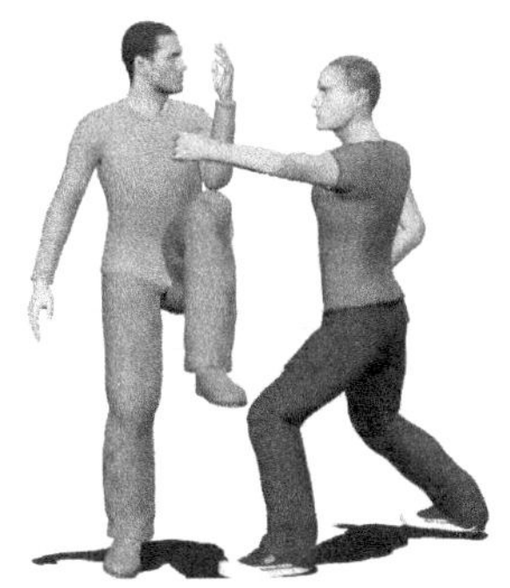

If the distance is too close to kick the defender stomps the knee with his left foot.

The defender chops the neck with his left hand.

The defender steps forward with his right foot, pushes the attacker's neck down and the attacker's left arm up and around (a spiral, not up or sideways) to execute a vertical arm pin.

Obviously, this defense can be used against a variety of kicks, in which case the defender can counter with his own (side) kick.

In the original karate the Imperial bodyguards didn't seem to have many kicks. And the kicks they did do were low, knee high. Today's modern students practice high kicks, but they should remember this point:

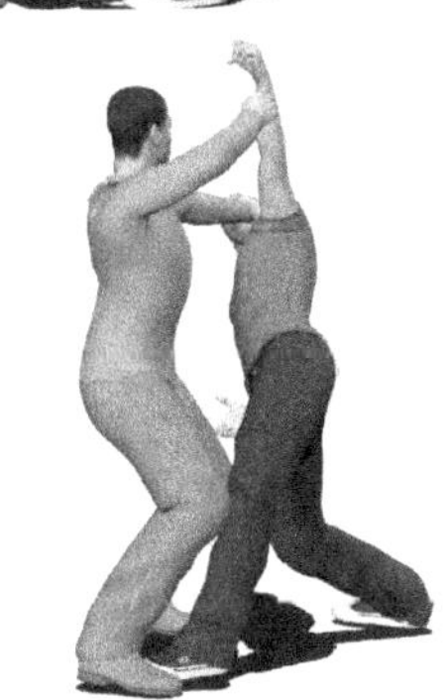

> In the dojo kick high.
> in the street kick low.

That way the karateka never risks loss of balance, or having his kick caught. Of course, if one is really good with kicks then this advice can be disregarded.

Open the left hand.

Execute a right crescent kick to the left palm.

Step through and set down in a horse stance with a right elbow to the left palm.

I was told that the crescent kick was for disarming a knife attack. I believed, and I practiced accordingly.

One day a friend expressed doubt as to the value of karate. 'What would you do if somebody had a knife?" He swung a tennis racket at me.

I used the crescent kick and blocked the racket, then demonstrated a strike to his face.

He was a bit surprised, and, tell the truth, so was I. All the practice and it had actually worked.

Many years later I came across more than one person opining that the crescent kick was useless for knocking a knife out of an opponent's hand. Obviously, they

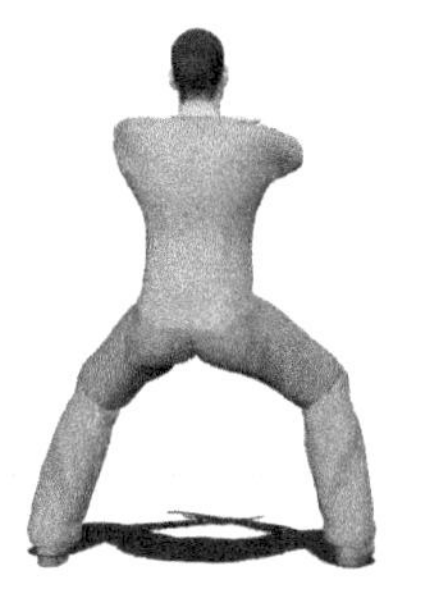

had not sufficient practice to make it work, and thus would degrade karate because of their own inadequacies.

Pinan Five
Application Nine

The attacker steps forward with the left foot and punches with the left hand. The defender steps back with the right foot into a back stance as he executes a right cross palm block.

The defender steps forward with the left foot as he pivots into a horse stance and executes a left punch to the nerve center under the attacker's left arm.

Other targets could be the floating rib, the pressure point one below and to the side of the nipple, or just the barrel of the body.

This technique uses all three elements of power, dropping the weight, thrusting the body, and turning the hips, thus making it extremely powerful.

If one thrusts his body in deeply he could execute a splitting move I call 'tripping the tiger,' as illustrated in the third illustration. This might be more appropriate at this level of the student's instruction.

Weightlifting: Conventional Karate-style

You decide to become a weight lifter. You set up ten stations. There is a station for squats, a station for curls, a station for presses, and so on. Then you do one repetition at each station, and that is your work out.

Sound silly, right? I mean, one rep? How can that work?

So you decide to do karate, and you do the form once. And you have a lot of forms so you do them all once. And then you move on.

How silly is that? That is like the weightlifting program I described above. Yet you would be shocked at how many people do that. They do the forms once or twice, then move on to the 'real stuff.'

Let me explain something.

A weightlifter might lift 100 pounds ten times, and he has lifted a thousand pounds.

If a karateka does the first move of his form ten times, he has lifted his body weight ten times, and if he weighs 150 pounds, that is 1,500 pounds!

And while the weight lifter moves from station to station, the karateka moves from posture to posture.

No, the karateka doesn't get bulky, he gets lean, he works off the fat, and he uses more than one isolated muscle. He uses all his muscles.

Now, don't mistake me, there are good reasons for weight lifting, but if you want to be karate strong, lean and fast and powerful, my brand of 'karate weightlifting' is much better.

I once had a fellow interested in a course of instruction, but first he had to 'get in shape.' I tried to make him understand about karate weightlifting, but he was stuck in stupidity. Can you believe it?

Chapter Thirty-Two
Pinan Five
(section four)

There is no place in contemporary Karate for different schools. Some instructors, I know, claim to have invented new and unusual kata, and so they arrogate to themselves the right to be called founders of "schools". Indeed, I have heard myself and my colleagues referred to as the Shotokan school, but I strongly object to this attempt at classification. My belief is that all these "schools" should be amalgamated into one, so that Karate may orderly progress into man's future. ~ Gichin Funakoshi

Pinan Five
section four

I added circles here. Raise the right hand and circle through a high block. Lower the left hand to circle through a low block.

Continue the circling of the hand to a left palm palm block and a right inward low block.

Continue the circling of the hands as you pivot into a low block with a right outward claw.

Raise the right knee as you spear with the left hand.

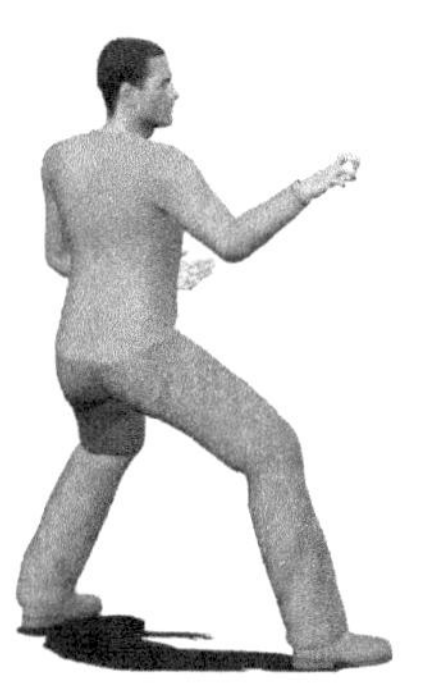

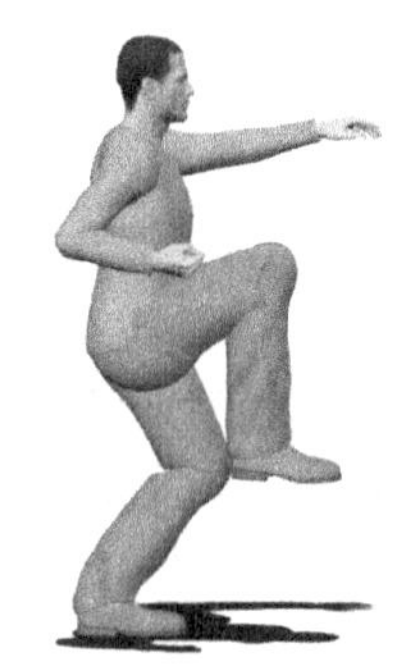

Pinan Five
Application Ten

The attacker steps forward with the left foot and punches with the left hand. The defender executes a left crescent kick to the inside of the wrist.

The defender sets down in a horse stance, holding the attacker's left wrist with his right hand he executes a horizontal elbow to the chest.

The defender executes a left elbow spike to the attacker's armpit.

The defender steps forward with the right foot and applies spiraling pressure (not up or back, but diagonally up) to the attacker's left arm, and downward spiraling pressure to the attacker's neck to execute a vertical arm pin.

This technique is unreal because of the distance between the attacker and the defender. One could, however, start at punching distance and leap back as he executes the crescent kick.

Or, one could just crescent kick the side of the attacker's head.

Pivot 180 degrees to the rear as you stomp the right foot. This is the supercharging movement. Simultaneously shoot the right fist upward. KIAI!

Do not put weight on a twisting joint. Move the body sufficient so that the joint is straight when the weight is shot through it.

Chapter Thirty-Three
Pinan Five
(section five)

The body should be able to change direction at any time. ~ Tatsuo Shimabuku

Pinan Five
section five

Bring the left foot back as you start lowering the arms.

Step forward with the right foot as you continue to lower the arms.

Bring the left foot behind the right foot in a cross stance as you execute a crossed wrist low block.

Step back with the left foot into a back stance as you begin circling the arms clockwise, the right hand circling through a high block and the left hand circling through a low block.

Usually there is a jump here, but if you jump you are trapped in a trajectory and unable to change. I prefer working on quick footwork.

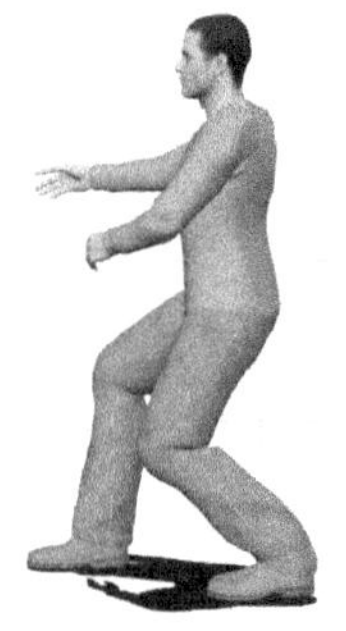

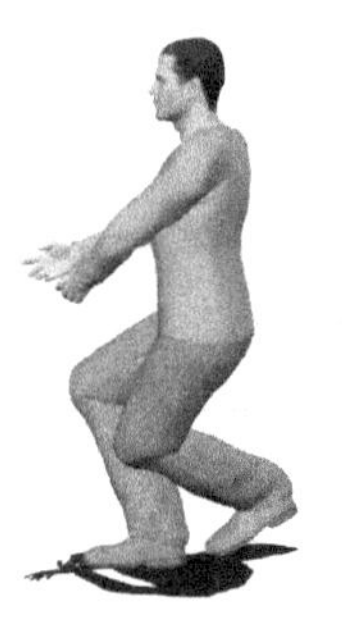

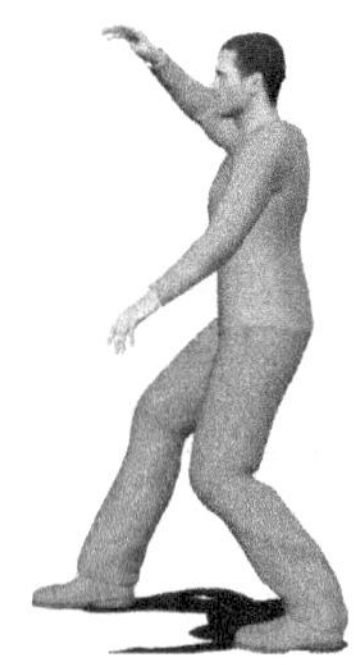

About the Jump

At this point in the form there is a jump. I don't do it.

Yes, I have seen all sorts of jumping over the low swing of the staff or sword, the kneeling under a second cut and pushing on the knee with a X block. And even climbing up the body of an opponent. And it all seems a bit much.

I usually teach people how to jump and duck with one of the first exercises I teach them. I simply swing a stick at them and they duck or jump or get hit. I describe this drill more fully in the section on freestyle.

In place of this jump I practice the quick pivot and the forward step.

Why do I do this? Well, I'm not going to tell you that jumping is worthless. I certainly don't believe that. And I believe there is a calisthenic to the move that builds certain muscles and body movements.

One day my instructor was invited to freestyle with a high ranking black belt from Korea. The Korean was a 7th black and Bob was a 6th black, so there was some sort of significance to it all. More than that, however, was the fact that Bob had a reputation and the fellow wanted to see if Bob was really that good, so he suggested a little match. This was at Bob's house in the Santa Cruz mountains.

The Korean did a big warm up session while Bob leaned against the railing of his porch and sipped a bit of rum and Coke. Bob's favorite drink. The Korean looked at Bob, was a little bit puzzled, and asked if Bob was going to warm up. Bob placed his drink on the railing and said, "I'm warm."

They faced off, and the very first technique out of the chute, the Korean jumped through the air with a beautiful flying spinning back kick. When he landed he found that he had missed. Also, he didn't know where Bob was. He looked around and found that while he was flying through the air Bob had simply walked around him.

The point is that while you are in the air you have no base, you can't change techniques or adapt. You are locked into a sequence and there's nothing you can do about it.

And that's why I rarely do jumping kicks. But this is NOT a judgement on kicks. Just make sure you practice them enough before using them.

Bring the right foot back (switch step) as you circle the left hand through a palm block and the right hand through an open hand inverted low block. This is the 'pole position.'

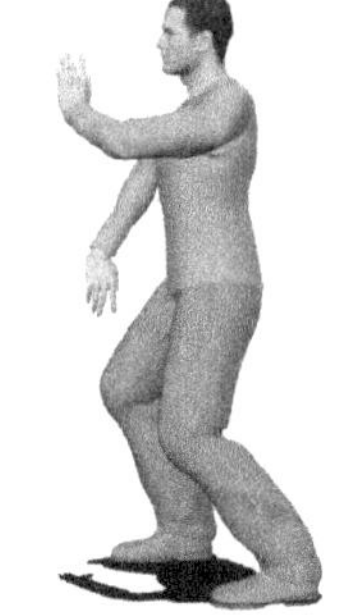

Step forward with the right foot into a front stance as you execute a right middle outward open hand block.

Move the left foot sideways behind the right foot, pivot 180 degrees to face in the opposite direction in a front stance as you execute a left palm block and a right palm up spear hand.

Pivot to the right into a front stance as you execute a right high level outward block with open palm face up. Simultaneously execute a left low block with open hand.

Pinan Five
Application Eleven

The attacker steps forward with the right foot and punches with the right hand. The defender steps back into a back stance with his left foot as he executes a right inward block.

The attacker punches with the left hand. The defender brings the left foot behind the right foot in an X stance as he executes a right augmented outward middle block.

The defender raises his right knee as he executes a left spear hand to the eyes.

The defender pivots 180 degrees and stomps his foot in a back stance as he executes a right punch to the chin of the attacker.

You can spear the eyes with either hand, and you can use the knee, and you can stomp on the attacker's foot with yours, and many other things.

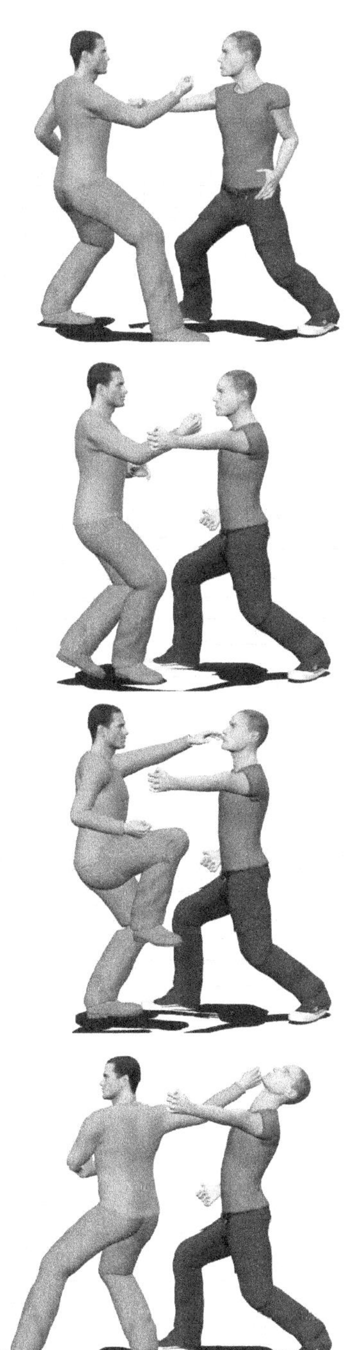

Bring the left foot back to the right foot.

Pivot to the left into an X stance with the right foot heel up. The right hand executes a low block and the left hand does an upper level outward block.

Step forward with the right foot into a front stance as you execute a right palm and a left spear hand, palm up to the groin area.

Pivot to the left into a front stance as you execute a right low block with open hand and a left upper level outward block.

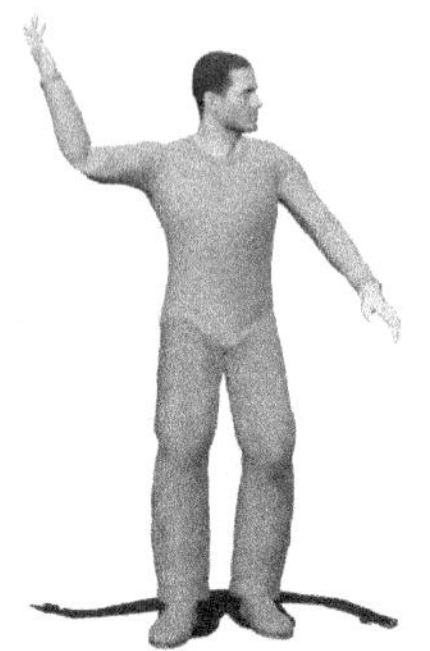

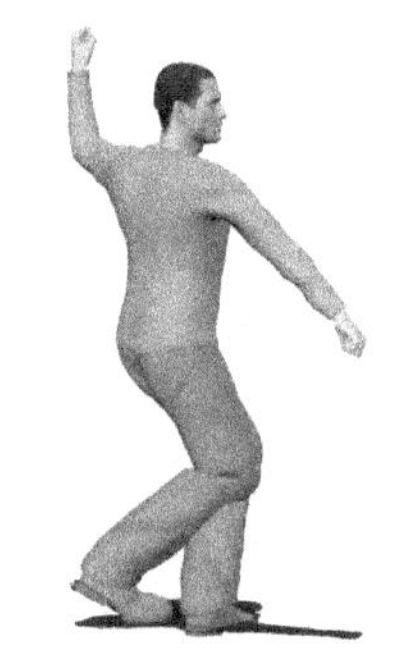

Pinan Five
Application Twelve

The attacker steps forward with the right foot and punches with the right hand. The defender moves forward with the left foot and closes the attacker's right arm with a left palm block. Simultaneously he strikes (or grabs) the groin with the right hand.

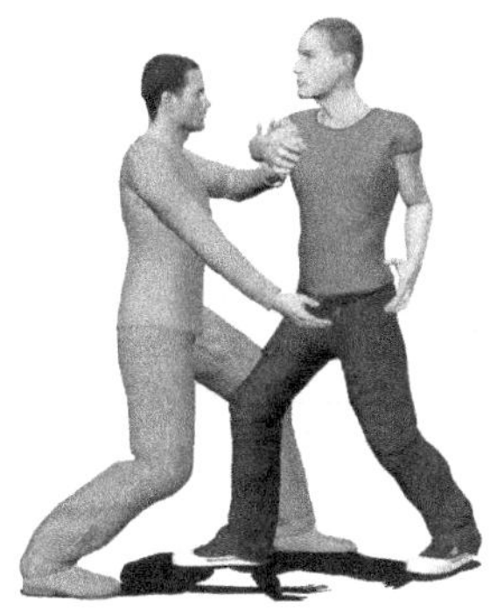

The defender pivots to the right into a horse stance as he traps the attacker's right arm with his right arm and breaks the attacker's elbow with this left arm. Note that the defender's left knee is breaking the stance, and possibly the right knee, of the attacker.

The defender shuffles into the attacker, keeping the right arm trapped and extending the left arm across the throat, thus affecting a 'splitting technique.'

Return to the natural stance.

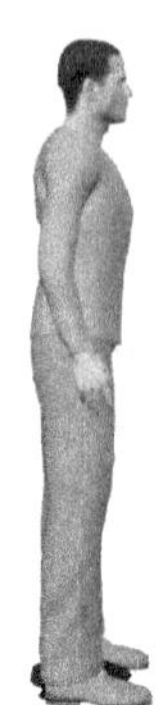

Pinan Five Application Thirteen

While this technique can be used for a punch, it is best used for a sword.

The attacker reaches across his body to draw his sword.

The defender steps forward with the right foot and presses the attacker's 'draw' hand against his body and grabs the attacker's sword with his other hand.

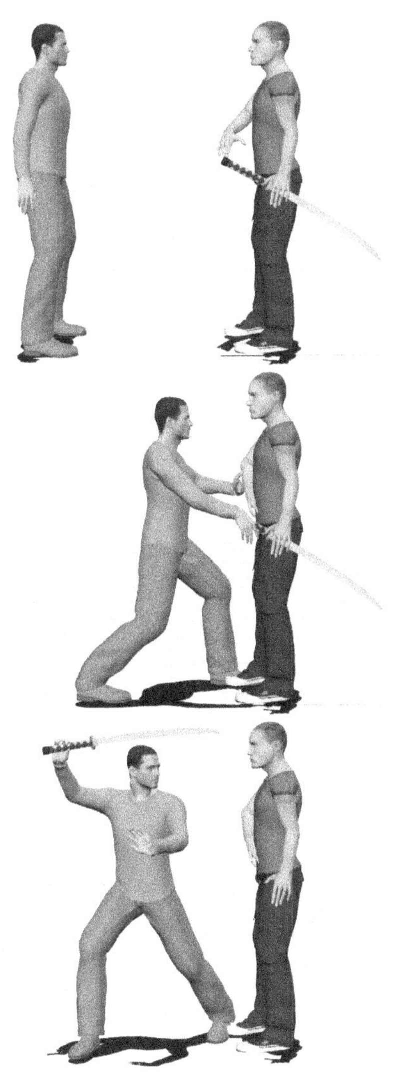

The defender then pivots in the other direction. He has pushed the attacker off balance, tied up his drawing hand, and should be able to draw the attacker's sword.

Consider that the Imperial bodyguards were weaponless, and they would have to defeat people with weapons. Doesn't it make sense that they would practice disarming the sword wielders? And this technique is perfect for that task.

I have found this to be a fairly misunderstood movement. In the Kang Duk Won we simply cross blocked a punch and grabbed the groin. The truth of this technique, when understood as a defense against weapons, is something more.

Circle of Blocks

One of the tools in Matrixing is the Circle of Blocks. These are the eight blocks which surround the body. If you understand and can use the eight blocks then you are an expert in Karate. Below is the circle of blocks. I have filled in the squares for each incoming attack with the self defense from Karate that would handle it. This tool is invaluable in analyzing how effective karate is, what blank spots it has, and so on.

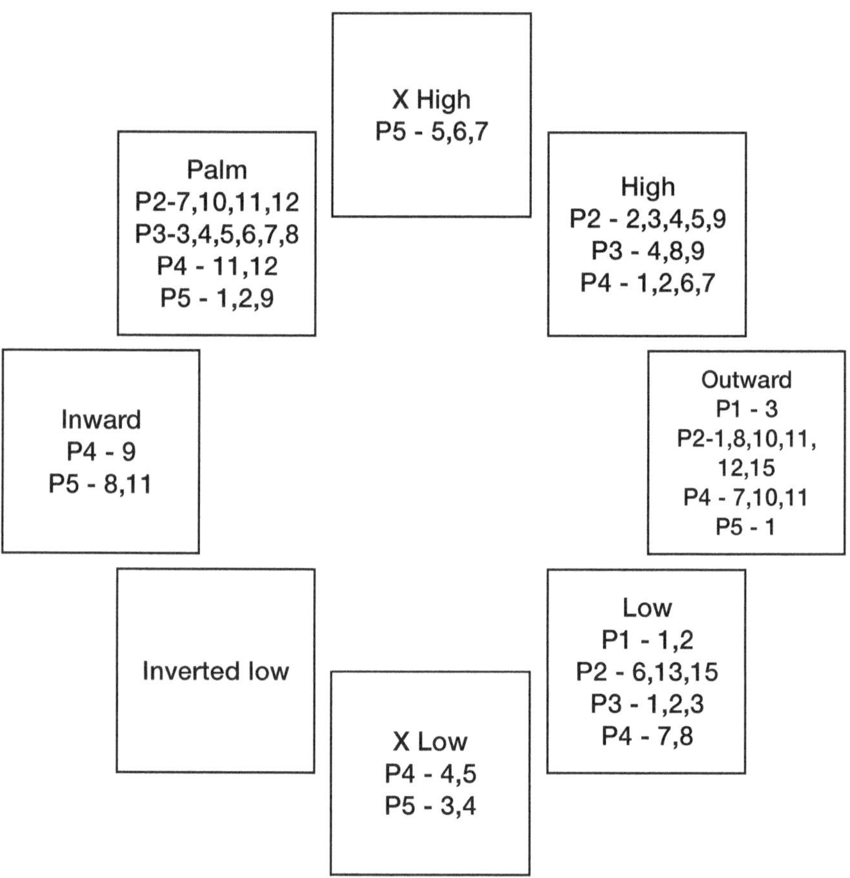

You can see that the squares are filled in fairly well, with the one exception being the inverted low block. The inverted low block, however, is found, but not exploited in many of the moves in the forms. It is also a big part of the Lop Sau exercise in the Freestyle drills.

You can see that karate is fairly well balanced. One would think that the art is weak in certain other areas, for instance grab arts. But you have seen the various joint locks and throws inherent in the techniques in this book.

The real problem with Karate is not in the techniques, or in the ranges of techniques, but in the way it has become specialized for striking only. This reflects the fact that instructors have catered to children and tournaments and so on.

Teachers didn't want to show the real techniques, grab arts were too difficult (and dangerous) to show to children, and so on.

At this point, understanding the potential workability of karate, and how realistic and usable the techniques can be, we are going to move into a second type of karate. Interestingly, it also claims to come from the White Crane Kung Fu lineage.

My opinion is that this type of karate, known as Pan Gai Noon in China, is even more workable, and can develop a truly polished practitioner.

The Alley

In the following section you will be coming across the concept of 'The Alley.'

The alley is when you raise your hands to the fighting position, midway between up and down, midway between forward and back, and pointing towards your opponent's shoulder.

Your hands can be faced outward, as if desiring peace. If the attacker punches between your hands he is 'in the alley,' or coming 'down the alley.' If he punches outside your hands he is 'outside the alley.'

Down the alley usually means he is punching straight, often a jab, and you should slap it past or aside.

Outside the alley means you should align your stance and body and use a harder block.

The alley segues into various fighting drills and concepts.

I mention it here so you will not be confused when you come across it in the following chapter.

I will delve deeper into it in the freestyle section later in the book.

Chapter Thirty-Four
Sanchin

Karate is the most Zen-like of all the Martial Arts. It has abandoned the sword. This means that it transcends the idea of winning and losing to become a way of thinking and living for the sake of other people in accordance with the way of Heaven. Its meanings, therefore, reach the profoundest levels of human thought.

…if the Budo is removed from karate, it is nothing more than sport karate, show karate or even fashion karate – the idea of training merely to be fashionable.

Karate that has discarded Budo has no substance. It is nothing more than a barbaric method of fighting or a promotional tool for the purpose of profit. No matter how popular it becomes, it is meaningless. ~ Mas Oyama

Below are the bonus videos for Sanchin.

sanchin front.mp4   https://youtu.be/8mwXdSy9p1k

sanchin side   https://youtu.be/VETDUQhAm3w

sanchin explanation.mp4   https://youtu.be/vBQtpIhzo5M

Sanchin

Many years ago, after having studied Karate for 20 years and thinking I knew a whole heck of a lot, some fellow told me:

If you don't know Sanchin you don't know Karate.

Now, wait a minute. After 20 years of practicing Karate somebody says I didn't know karate?

What a bozo, eh?

But, curiosity nibbling at me, I began to research Sanchin. And, after a couple of years of nibbling, I realized he was right!

The problem was there were no real workable techniques in the form.

So I began examining the various incarnations of Sanchin.

I took apart Hangetsu. Workable blocks, but…stiff and unusable. It was a technique form the way Shotokan did it, but the techniques were nothing but stiff basics. Nothing there. Or, there were better forms that taught the basics better.

I looked at Goju Ryu. Deep, gasping, raucous breathing. Sounded like they were trying to whistle through their, uh, bottom part.

I looked at Uechi, which was closer to the historical source of the form. Tremendous power, dynamic tension, but…not workable.

Shotokan broke it into basics, redundant basics. Goju made it into a breathing form. Uechi made it into a muscle form.

I knew I was missing the essence. The form had been translated, reconfigured, moved from here to there, and I knew I wasn't seeing the real Sanchin.

I began to trace it through China, to the White Crane style of Kung Fu. The originator of White Crane Kung Fu was Fang Qiniang. A girl.

And I realized, thunder boomed and lightening struck me and rain washed through my brain, that a woman would NOT be into muscles, harsh breathing, or hard techniques that would jar the bones.

A woman, especially one who was making swift but soft waving movements of her hands based on the waving wings of a crane, would move… differently.

I began *really* examining at the form.

Sanchin is basically one move repeated nine times, a few finger thrusts, then that one move repeated, with a palm style low block, three more times.

One technique. Twelve times.

But everybody said the form was core, mystical, mysterious, chi building… and so on.

And nobody actually looked at the hand motion of the one, single technique which is the heart of Sanchin.

I did.

And instead of using the edges of hands, to block or even to 'guide' I reconfigured the basic technique as a simple slap and grab.

Other versions of the form taught a person to sink the weight and become stiff and unyielding, to be pounded upon and 'take it.'

What woman would do that?

A woman would make a fan like motion with one hand, and delicately grasp with the second hand.

Yes, she would develop strength, and use stances, but she wouldn't be wanting to take full force body strikes. That's for those silly men who *like* to get hit.

So here is Sanchin the way a girl might do it, as imagined by the unsettled mind of Al Case.

Sanchin

From a standing position take a 'moon' step. That is the right foot comes halfway in to the body and makes a circle to a position one foot length in front of the left foot. Simultaneously shoot a double spear hand downward to the front.

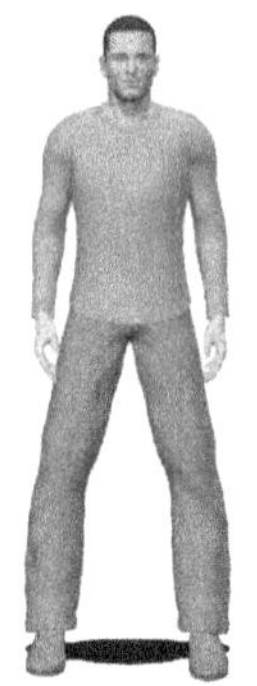

Bring the hands inward and scoop them up on the center line of the body.

Overturn the hands as you execute double outward grabbing.

It is important that each step you take is dedicated to sinking the weight into the ground, and creating an energy connection with the ground.

A Breakdown of the Slap Grab Concept

If a fly is buzzing about, trying to land on your nose, would you do a powerful high block?

No.

You would swat it. You would…slap it. So slapping is actually the first of all karate techniques. You usually have a slap before you do a block, but everybody just thinks of the slap as a motion to counter the motion of the block, and they totally miss the fact that the slap is a valid first and instinctive and intuitive response for a fly, and even for a fist.

The second thing one does is to grasp. As if to grab.

And the third thing would be to use the closed fist of the grasp to block.

Can you see what happened to karate?

Everybody missed the slap, put it aside, in favor of the 'power' of the closed fist.

But the slap is first, the grab is second, and the block is third, in terms of body motion, and therefore in terms of usable self defense.

Everybody started looking for the POWER! And missed the soft, girlish motion of the slap.

Oh, we've come a long way, baby, but most of the journey has been on the wrong path.

Execute a left palm block as you retract the right hand.

Execute a right outward grabbing block.

Execute a left punch. The hips should turn slightly so that the punch has the weight of the whole body behind it.

Retract the punching hand to the double outward grabbing position.

Your hips should be making subtle shifts with every motion to ensure body alignment, and that the energy of the grounding is going through the body.

The Perfect Technique

This is the one technique done in Sanchin (and Seisan).

The student assumes a sanchin stance and scoops his hands up the center and moves them outward. The hands should be bent slightly outward.

The student moves the left hand across the body in a palm block as he scoops the right hand across the mid-section.

The student continues the circular motion of the right hand to an outward middle 'grab.' The left hand is palm down in a 'grab.'

The student punches with the left hand.

This sequence is repeated nine times, then three times with the addition of a low palm block added before the technique.

So the student is taught to lock his stance down, to move while keeping his gravity down, to move his hips slightly to align the body, and to slap an attack away and then grasp it.

Just like the form as I have reworked it here.

Take a moon step. Sink the weight. Your body should be taut, but not tight. You should be able to take a punch not by focusing muscle, but by focusing energy.

Execute a right palm block as the left hand retracts.

Execute a left outward grabbing block. The right hand should be in a grabbing position at the left elbow.

Execute a right punch, turning the hips slightly into the punch.

The Double Outward Grabbing Concept

The attacker pushes, and the defender brings his arms up the centerline and moves them outward.

The elbows are in so an incoming force will slip off, and so the energy is based on the tan tien.

The hands are bent outward to GRIP the attacker.

This is a simple stopping motion that establishes control, and can be followed up with punches, elbows, knees kicks, or even grab arts.

It will segue into a Slap/Grab intuitively.

It synchronizes perfectly with the 'Alley Theory' of fighting, which I will explain in the freestyle section.

Retract the punching hand to the double outward grabbing position.

Take a moon step, sinking the weight into the ground. Make sure you are firm and relaxed before executing the next move.

Execute a left palm as you retract the right hand.

Execute a right outward grabbing block.

If you examine the circling of the hands you will understand that you are describing two circles, the palm block goes across the body and the grabbing block circles out from the body. It is very important to study this circling sequence, for if you practice it with dedication you will certainly see the yin yang in it. If you have trouble seeing the yin yang you should do the form with closed eyes. The mind will see much better than the eyes.

Using a Single Outward Grab

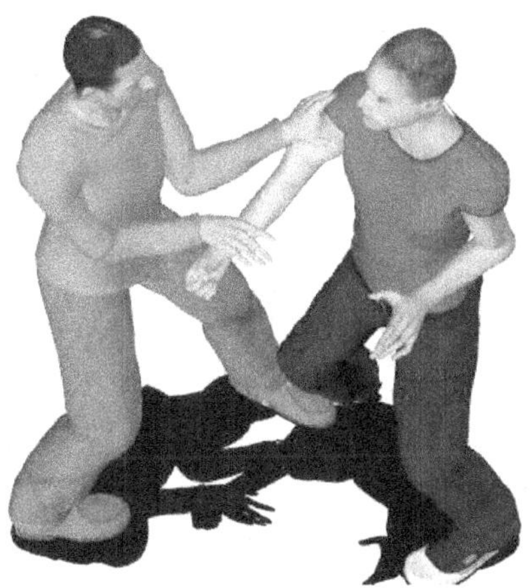

Sanchin trains not to block, but to grab.

It is not destroying somebody with mindless violence, it is controlling them with subtle movements.

If you look at the hand positions you may be able to find some very interesting and workable pressure points.

And, if you look at potential techniques you can find some interesting grab arts.

Execute a left punch. Turn the hips slightly into the punch and back.

Retract the punching hand.

Step to the left with the right foot, turning 180 degrees and facing in the other direction. The right foot should be on a toe to heel line with the left foot. This will stop the hips from gyrating when you turn. Some people say you should step, crossing the feet, then turn. I usually just step/turn in one movement. Crossing the legs isn't great strategy, and it takes extra time.

Thus far there have been three sequences.

Slap/grab and punch with the right foot forward.

Slap/grab and punch with the left foot forward.

Slap/grab and punch with the right foot forward.

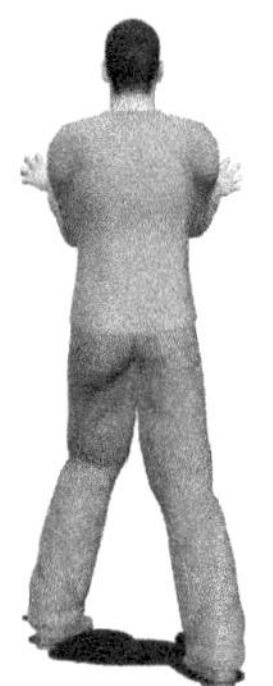

Basic Slap Grab Technique

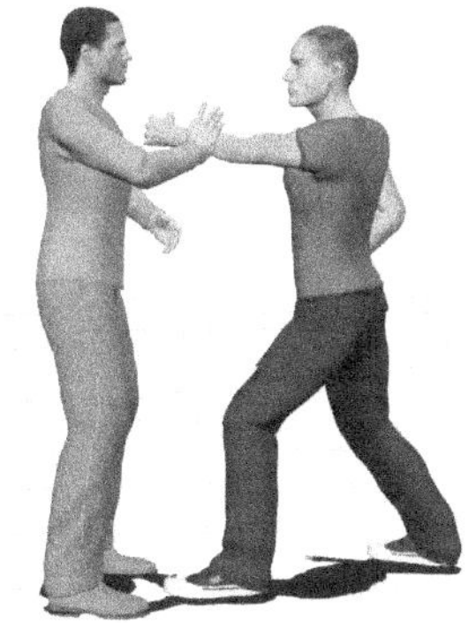

Here is how the slap grab technique works.

The attacker steps forward and punches. The defender slaps the punch inward.

The defender grabs the attackers left wrist with his left hand.

The defender pulls with the left hand as he strikes with the right hand.

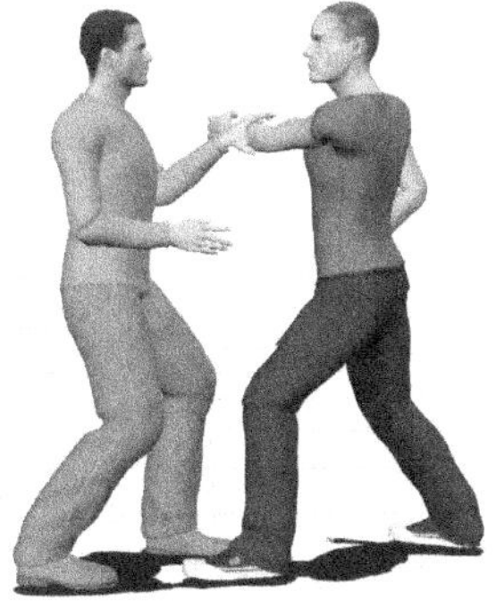

This is powerful and simple.

With a little practice you will be shocked at how quickly this technique works.

You can matrix the technique perfectly: it will work for closing the attacker (pushing his arm across his body) or opening (pushing his arm outward from his body.).

You can add the low palm block for a kick, then matrix the punches.

You can make this a two punch attack and slap the first punch and grab the second punch.

Once turned you must do the sequence four times to the rear.

Slap/grab and punch with the left foot forward.
Slap/grab and punch with the right foot forward.
Slap/grab and punch with the left foot forward.
Slap/grab and punch with the right foot forward.

When you finish the fourth step your right foot should be forward and ready for the 180 degree turn, as in the top figure on this page.

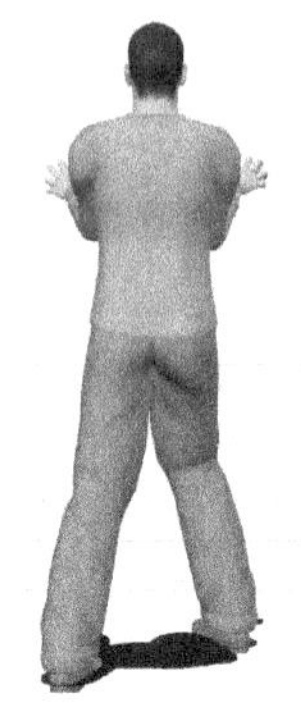

Step to the left with your right foot and sink the weight into a Sanchin stance. The hands should be in the double outward grabbing position, as in the second figure.

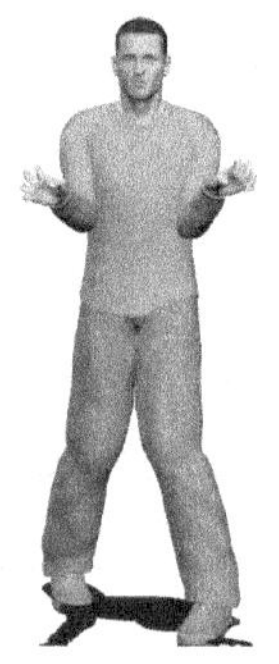

Slap with the right hand as in figure 3.

Grab with the left hand as in figure 4.

Sink the weight and make sure you are connected to the ground before you do the technique. Eventually, when you have mastered this move, you can do the steps and sink and technique all at once. But time spent isolating these basic-basics is time well spent. After over 50 years of practicing the arts I still work on this sinking then striking sequence.

Double Slap Grab Technique

The attacker punches with the left hand. The defender slaps it closed with the right hand.

The attacker punches with the right hand. The Defender stops it by grabbing the biceps.

The Defender pulls with the left hand and punches with the right.

Make sure you turn the hips slightly to the right in the second image so they will align with the feet.

Make sure you turn the hips slightly to the left when you execute the punch so as to put the whole body behind the punch.

You can, instead of ending the attack with a punch, allow the attacker to keep punching, and you keep doing the slap grab. This is wonderful for a stepping drill.

Back and forth across the room, the attacker coming 'down the alley,' and, every once in a while, 'outside the alley.'

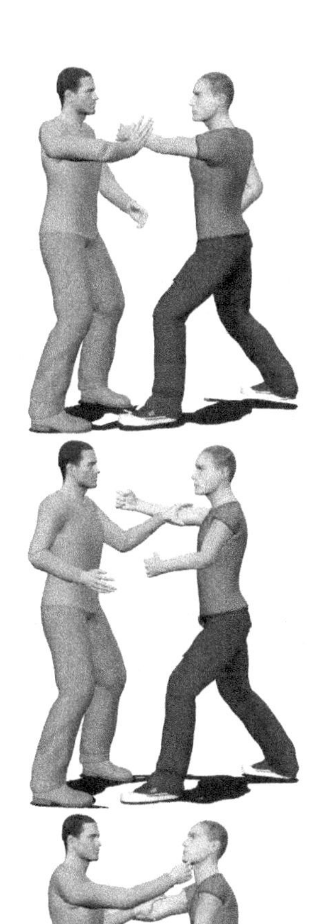

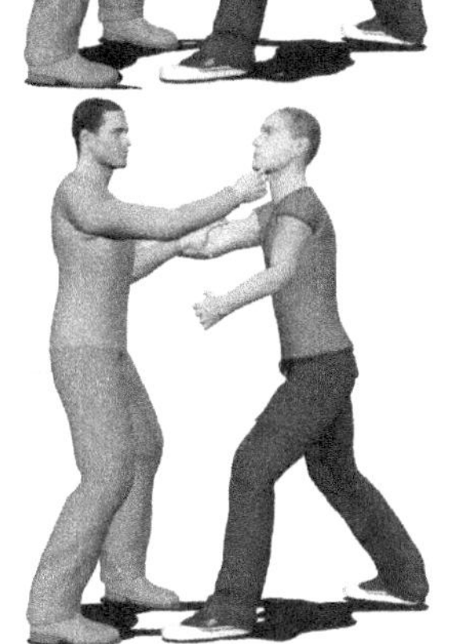

Execute a right punch.

Retract the hands to double outward grabbing blocks.

Take a moon step with the left foot.

Execute a right palm block as you retract the left hand.

Focus on the muscles in your legs to turn and put your hips into each move.

Matrixing the Basic Slap Grab Technique
(One punch)

Here are the four basic single punches that can be handled by the Basic Slap Grab Technique.

1) If the attacker punches with the right hand slap with the right hand and grab with the left hand.

2) If the attacker punches with the right hand slap with the left hand and grab with the right hand.

3) If the attacker punches with the left hand slap with the right hand and grab with the left hand.

4) If the attacker punches with the left hand slap with the left hand and grab with the right hand.

You will find differences between opening and closing techniques. Closing is always better, it evades force instead of meeting it straight on, but you'd better be able to make the opening technique work.

If the person doesn't punch on a straight enough line then his punch is more circular, he is going 'outside the alley' of your hands. This means you don't slap grab, you just raise a block and let him run into it.

Once you have the basic Slap Grab for a single punch down you should explore it for two punches and start looking for grab arts.

Execute a left outward grabbing block.

Execute a right punch, turning the hips slightly.

Retract the punch to the double outward grabbing position.

Retract both hands as fists as you expand the chest. This is going to be a waving motion of the whole chest and will give you extra power and enable to focus on breathing, sinking, and pulsing power.

Understanding the Slap Grab Matrix

The slap grab matrix is designed to handle people coming 'down the alley' of two raised hands. When they go outside of the alley you simply raise a hard block and let them run into your arm, which is energetically linked through your aligned body to planet earth.

When you pass the punch you are closing them.
When you open the punch you are stopping them, with a grab or a hard block.
This leads to four potentials of inside/outside. When you slap grab two strikes the options are:

in/in
in/out
out/in
out/out

Understanding this concept will help you understand the slap grab, make it easier to learn, and make it more effective to use.

Shoot both hands to the front in double spears. the fingers may be splayed slightly. You will be doing this three times.

Retract the hands and expand the chest.

Spear the hands as you wave the body back to the original position.

Retract the hands as fists and expand the chest.

The spearing movement is not so much a strike as a release of power. Your hands should be focused but they are also 'throwing' energy.

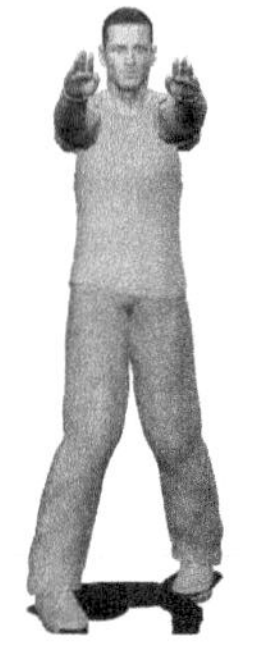

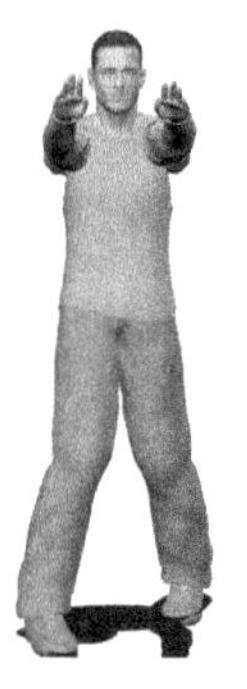

Matrixing the Basic Slap Grab Technique
(Two Punches)

Here are the four basic double punches that can be handled by the Basic Slap Grab Technique.

1) If the attacker punches with the right hand slap with the right hand and pass the second punch with the left hand.

2) If the attacker punches with the right hand slap with the left hand and grab the second punch with the right hand.

3) If the attacker punches with the left hand slap with the right hand (pass) and pass the second punch with the left hand.

4) If the attacker punches with the left hand slap with the left hand (pass) and grab the second punch with the right hand.

If you stop the first punch then pass the second one you will usually have to move back out of range for the pass.

If the person doesn't punch on a straight enough line then his punch is more circular, he is going 'outside the alley.' This means you don't slap/grab, you just raise a block and let him run into it.

Once you have the basic Slap Grab for a double punch down you should look for grab arts.

Spear the hands to the front.

Step straight back with the left foot as you point the fingers in the direction you are stepping, which will enable you to have more snap and focus.

Bring the right foot to the position the left foot was in before it moved. Execute a left low palm bock and cover the face with the right hand.

Execute a left outward grabbing block.

The low block move is not a sink your weight, then do the technique. You should be sinking the weight as you execute the downward palm.

This move, and the two immediately following, to the rear (180 degrees) and then 90 degrees to the front, are done as if on a square.

Low Block Slap Grab
Technique One

The attacker kicks with the left foot. The defender executes a right palm block to the shin.

The rest of the technique is obviously from Basic Slap Grab Technique from a few pages ago.

The attacker sets down with punches with the left hand. The defender closes the punch with a right slap.

The defender grabs the attacker's left hand with his right hand.

The defender executes a right punch.

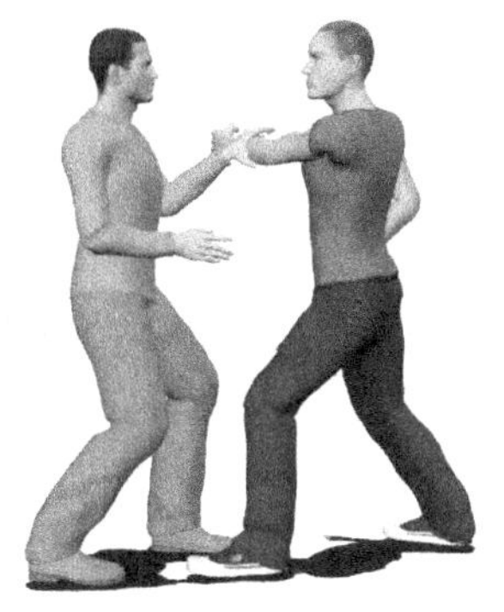

To get the full flavor of this technique return to the section on matrixing punches and apply, the matrix for a two punch slap grab defense. Matrix the right hand opening and closing, and the left hand opening and closing.

Make sure you matrix the kick, blocking it with the right hand, with the left hand, then having your partner attack with the other leg.

Execute a right punch, turning the hips slightly to align the body.

Retract the punch to a double outward grab position.

Step to the rear, directly behind the left foot, with the right foot. Point the fingers in the direction you are going to enhance your snap and focus.

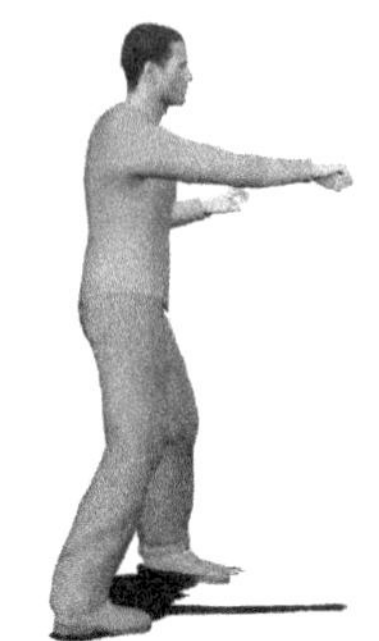

Sink your weight into a Sanchin stance facing in the opposite direction as you execute a right low palm block and cover the face with the left palm.

The hand covering the face is a slap, part of the slap/grab sequence. The rhythm of this movement does not lend itself to a smooth slap grab, so we make it a cover. I played with this concept heavily, and I suggest you look at it, too. It will help your understanding of how to adjust the rhythm in a real confrontation.

Low Block Slap Grab
Technique Two

The defender kicks with the left foot. The defender executes a right palm block to the shin.

The rest of the technique is obviously the Basic Slap Grab Technique for Two Punches we discussed earlier in this chapter.

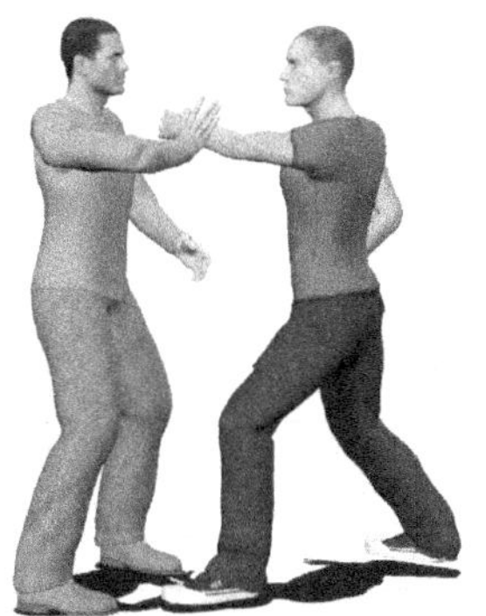

The attacker sets down and punches with the right hand. The defender closes the punch with a right slap.

The attacker punches with the right hand. The defender stops the punch with a left grab to the biceps.

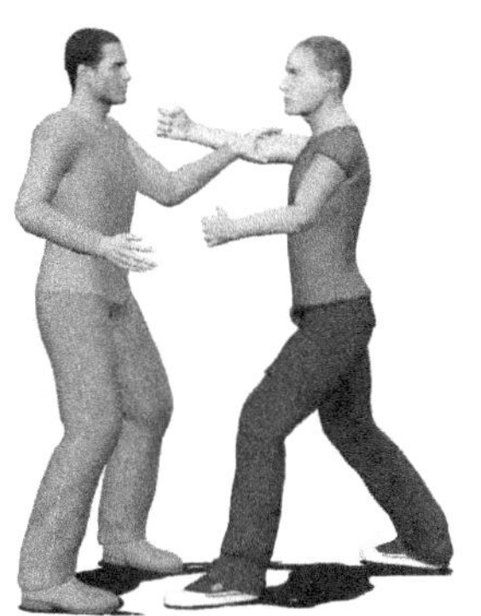

The defender executes a right punch.

Again, matrix everything.
Matrix blocking the kick with the right hand closing and opening.
Matrix a right/left punch, opening and closing.
Matrix a right/left punch closing and opening.
Matrix with the first punch being delivered with the left hand, and so on.

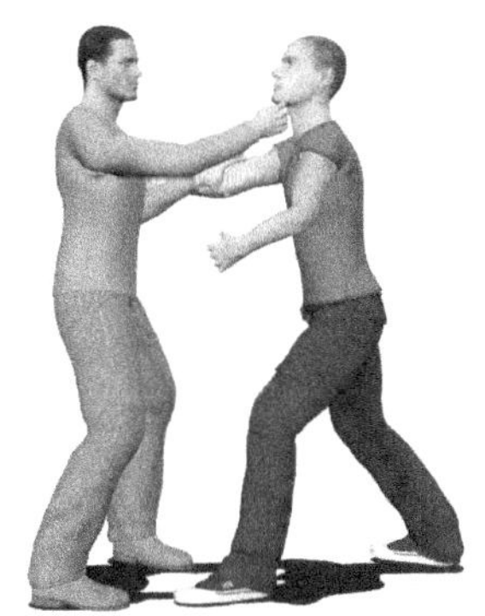

You will likely get confused, so start writing out the attacks and defenses.

Execute a right outward grabbing block.

Execute a left punch, turning the hips slightly.

Retract the punch to the double outward grabbing position.

Step directly back with the left foot as you point the fingers in the direction you are going. Pointing the fingers sets up the snap, and thereby the focus.

The Matrix of the Perfect Technique

Use a right low palm block and a left slap and right grab for the following four techniques.

right kick right punch
right kick left punch
left kick right punch
left kick left punch

Use a right low palm block and a right slap and left grab for the following four techniques.

right kick right punch
right kick left punch
left kick right punch
left kick left punch

Use a left low palm block and a left slap and right grab for the following four techniques.

right kick right punch
right kick left punch
left kick right punch
left kick left punch

Use a left low palm block and a right slap and left grab for the following four techniques.

right kick right punch
right kick left punch
left kick right punch
left kick left punch

Some of these techniques might be awkward, but they can all be made to work, and that is the secret: to not just look at the list and say, 'Oh, I understand that, and I've done enough work so I don't need to practice,' but rather to make yourself do the work. Explore each specific technique, make notes as to which is viable, which is weak, which needs work, which angles need to be corrected, and so on.

Sink into a Sanchin stance as you execute a left low palm block with the left hand and cover the face with the right palm.

Execute a left outward grabbing block.

Execute a right punch.

Retract the punch to the double outward grabbing position.

Sanchin and Seisan

Sanchin

Sanchin is a power form. This is because one must sink the weight, become unmovable, and learn to generate power.

Power is generated through the sinking of the stance, which creates work, which makes the tan tien (the body energy generator) work harder.

People used to spend a couple of years just walking in Sanchin to learn how to do this. With the theory presented here it need not take years, BUT…one must apply the theory. Understand it and work it until it works.

Seisan

The second form, in the following chapter, is Seisan, and I always call it the technique form. This is because it is nothing but variations on the first technique.

The third form, Sanseirui, was labeled a 'demonstration' form by Kanbun Uechi, (according to the book by Mattson) who put together the Uechi Ryu system out of Pan Gai Noon.

Yet there may be value in the form. It does expand a bit into other areas, and it does present a different footwork. And footwork, even if you are a big, strong, powerful man, is what a frail, girl might be in need of. Especially when showing her system to the powerful kung fu men of the day.

Return to the beginning position.

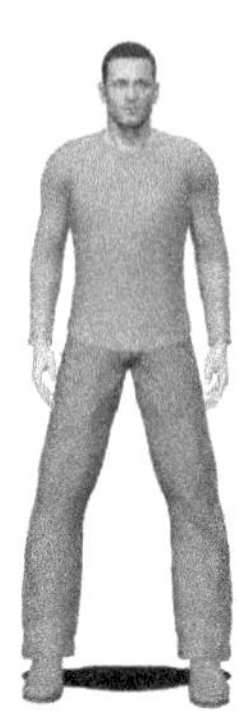

Chapter Thirty-Five
Seisan
(section one)

You must decide if karate is for your health or to aid your duty. ~ Anko Itosu

Below are the bonus videos for Seisan.

seisan front.mp4   https://youtu.be/6bbuHjCd9_c

seisan side   https://youtu.be/7e_mw0_17NI

seisan explanation.mp4   https://youtu.be/xym1-9dr4T4

Seisan
section one

Start from a natural stance.

Bring the left foot (half moon step) as you execute parries with both hands.

Step out with the left foot into an hourglass stance as you execute face high double ridge hands.

Retract the right hand slightly in a beak as you configure the left hand in a palm.

The beak can be a beak, or it can actually be a guiding hand, pulling an attack inward as you strike with the palm.

Seisan
Application One

The attacker begins an aggressive action.

The defender executes double ridge hand strikes to the attacker's neck.

The defender pulls the attacker's head down and executes a knee strike.

One can easily apply the double parry before striking with the ridge hands.

One can strike the ears with palms, the temples with ridge hands, the temples with thumb knuckles, and so on.

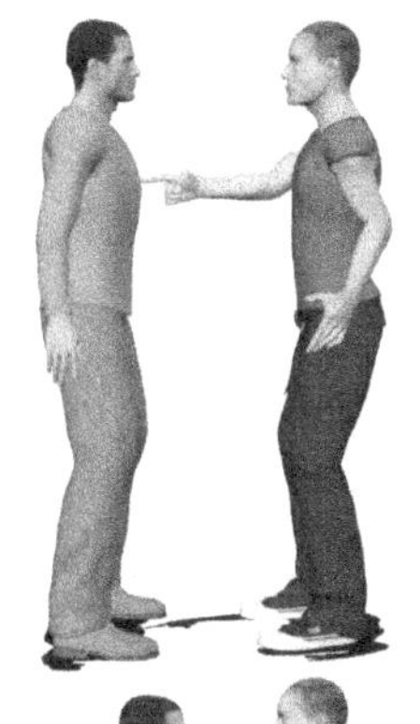

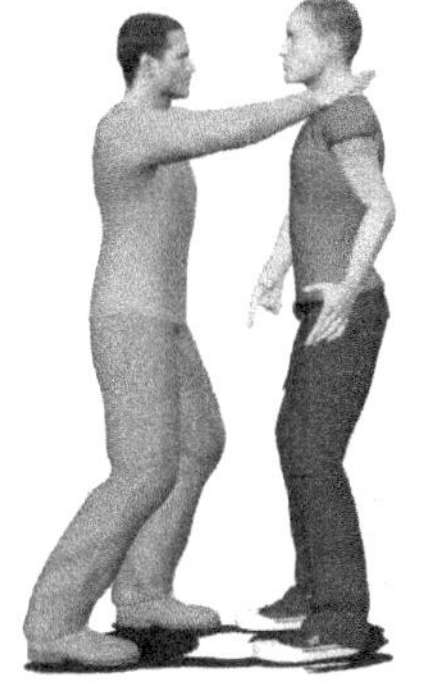

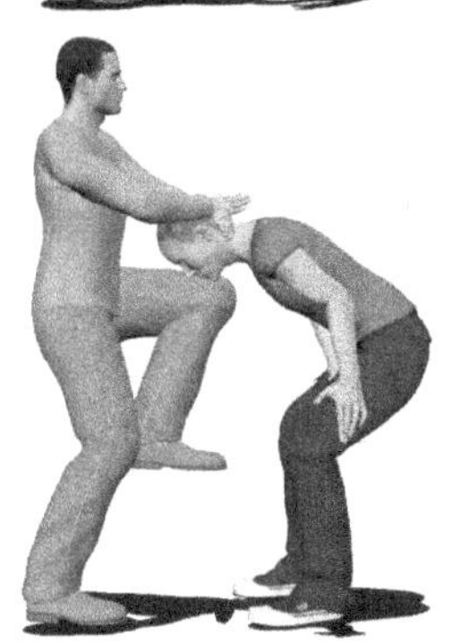

Retract the left hand in a beak as you execute a right palm strike.

Retract the right hand in a beak as you execute a left palm strike.

Retract the left hand in a beak as you execute a right pam strike.

Raise both hands in beaks.

Seisan
Application Two

The attacker steps forward and punches to the face with the right hand. The defender executes a left beak block.

The defender hooks and pulls the attacker's right hand with his left beak. Simultaneously he executes a right palm strike to the face.

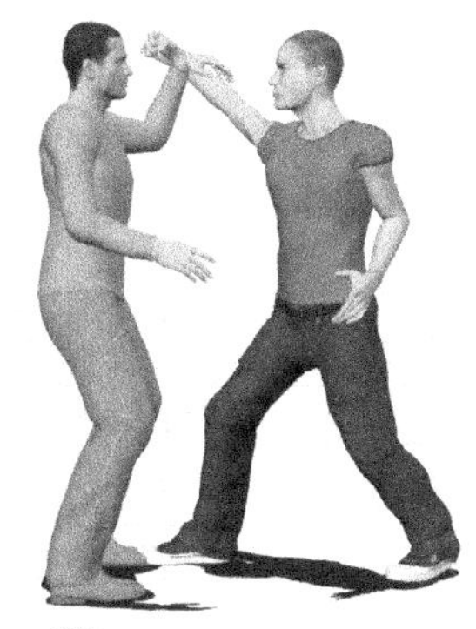

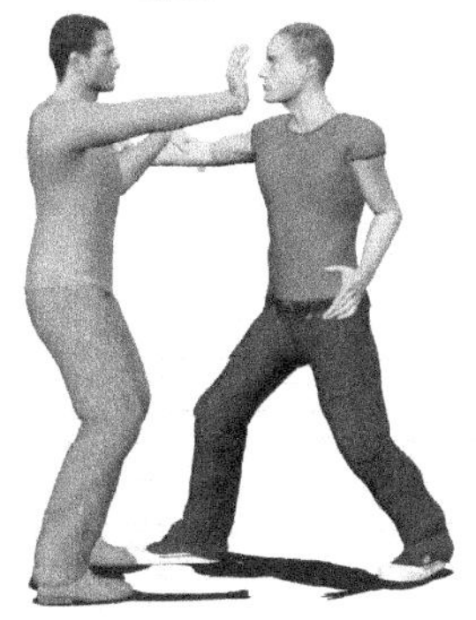

Secondary strikes can easily be handled by waving the hands to block with beak or palm.

For instance, a face strike with the left hand calls for a right beak and left palm.

A body strike with the left hand calls for a right parry.

Also, the student should be approaching the point where he isn't blocking so much as catching and guiding.

Bring both hands down to the right knee.

Set forward with the right foot in an hourglass stance. The right foot should be on a line with the left toes. The left hand executes a claw to the groin level. The right hand executes a claw to the groin area of an attacker behind him.

The hourglass stance is designed for the student to be able to resist pushes from the sides, and also from the front or rear.

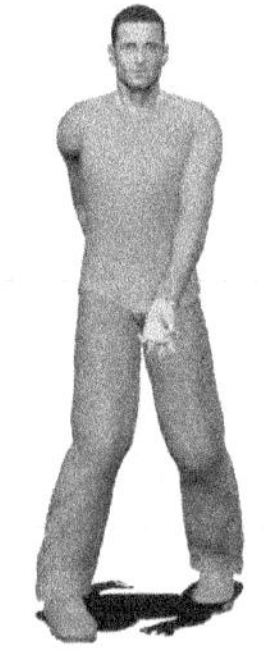

Chapter Thirty-Six
Seisan
(section two)

Secret techniques begin with basic techniques; Basic techniques end as secret techniques. There are no secrets at the beginning, but there are secrets at the end. The key to success is hard training ~ Mas Oyama

Seisan
section two

Step in front of the left foot with the right foot and turn to the rear into an hourglass stance. The left hand hand executes a claw to the groin area. The right hand executes a claw to the groin area of an attacker behind him.

Execute a left outward grabbing block.

Step with the right foot through a moon step (right foot comes in and goes out in a half circle into an hourglass stance). The right hand hand executes a claw to the groin area. The left hand executes a claw to the groin area of an attacker behind him.

Execute a right outward grabbing block.

Seisan
Application Three

The attacker grabs the defender in a bear hug from the rear.

The defender sinks his weight to protect his balance and executes a left claw to the groin.

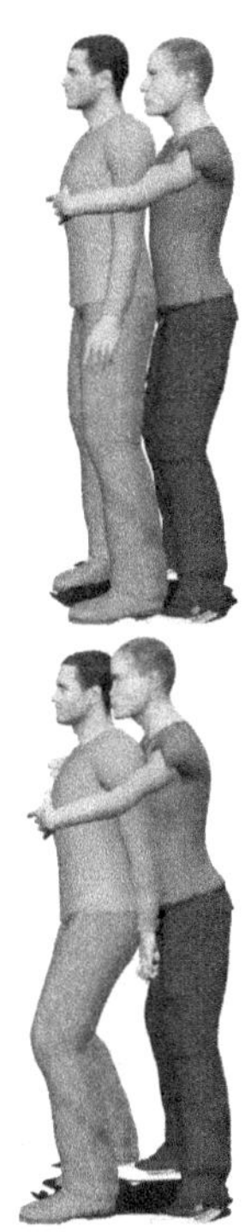

This is an important technique that eventually won't have much use. The fact is that karate builds a sixth sense. The karateka should, within a short time, begin feeling people attacking from the rear.

Still, it is useful for beginners, and should be practiced just so people can learn to sink their weight and retain their ground during up close and personal attacks.

Step with the left foot through a moon step into an hourglass stance. The left hand hand executes a claw to the groin area. The right hand executes a claw to the groin area of an attacker to the rear.

Execute a left outward grabbing block.

Bring the hands to the chamber position as you expand the chest. This creates a wave of energy through the body.

Shuffle forward, left foot then right foot, into an hourglass stance as you executes double spear hands downward.

Seisan
Application Three

The attacker grabs the defender in a bear hug from the front.

The defender sinks his weight to protect his balance and executes a right claw to the groin.

Make sure you head butt, bite, grind your chin into his eye socket, and so on.

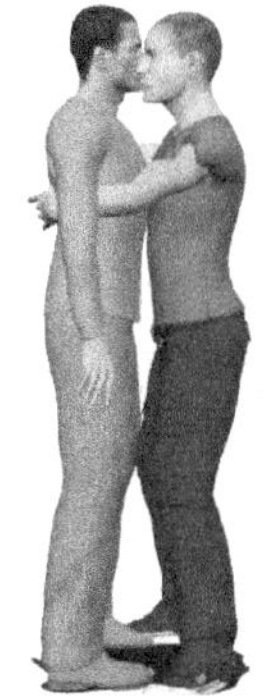

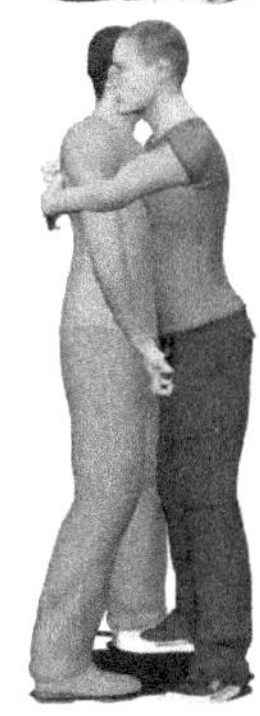

These two figures are a side view of the last two figures.

Note that the expansion of the chest is a wave form for the whole body.

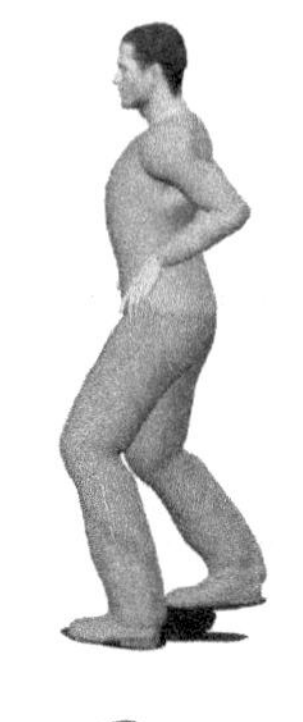

Chapter Thirty-Seven
Seisan
(section three)

There are many kinds of martial arts, …at a fundamental level these arts rest on the same basis. It is no exaggeration to say that the original sense of Karate-Do is at one with the basis of all martial arts. Form is emptiness, emptiness is form itself. The kara of Karate-Do means this. ~ Gichin Funakoshi

Seisan
section three

Step back and turn to the right into an hour glass stance as you circle the right hand through a high block and the left hand through an inverted low block.

Continue the circling of the hands to a left outward grab. The right hand circles to the inverted low block position.

Step forward with the right foot into a front stance as you execute a right vertical (upward) elbow strike with a beak configuration of the hand. Hold the left outward grab.

Retract the right foot to the hourglass position as you execute a left palm block and scoop the right hand across the body.

Seisan
Application Four

The attacker steps forward with the left foot and punches to the face with the left hand. The defender sinks his weight and executes a right high block.

The attacker punches with the right hand. The defender catches the attacker's right arm with his left outward grab. His right hand is circling down, staying in front of the attacker's left hand.

The defender steps forward with the right foot as he pulls on the left hand and executes a right vertical elbow strike.

This technique can easily be expanded.
Poke fingers into the eyes.
Move in with the right leg (you can be on the inside or outside of the attacker's left leg) to affect a split, and so on.

Execute a right outward grab.

Execute a left palm strike.

Execute a right palm block as you scoop the left hand across the body.

Execute a left outward grab.

Seisan
Application Five

This is a double slab/grab technique. You can do it with two slap grabs, or just two grabs as I show it.

The attacker executes a right punch, the defender catches it with a left outward grab and executes a right palm strike to the face.

The attacker executes a left punch, the defender catches it with a right outward grab and executes a left punch to the face.

You can also have the attacker deliver four punches, and you do two slap/grabs.

When you handle attacks with a continuous stream of slap/grabs the attacker will finally realize he can't get through the slap grabs so he punches around the hands in an outside circle. He has now gone outside the alley and presented his face. He has become TOTALLY predictable. When the defender sees this he will develop intuition.

Execute a right vertical fist.

Most karate strikes are horizontal fists. Horizontal fists are good for teaching children how to snap the wrists. However, turning the wrist on impact is a very bad idea. You don't want to load weight onto a twisting joint.

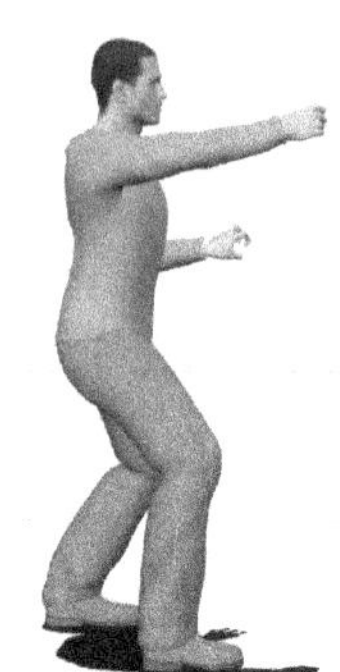

The vertical fist is called (in China) a 'Sun' fist. This, so I've been told, is because if you punch sand with a vertical fist it will leave the impression of the hieroglyphic for the word sun. I have no idea how true this is, or what 'sun' would mean in this instance. But…?

The vertical fist takes more practice to create snap, and you have to learn how to rely on closing the fingers fast enough to create that snap.

Chapter Thirty-Eight
Seisan
(section four)

Many Karate teachers teach a watered down style – no hip action and no depth of punching – so it is easy to say that these teachers have no depth to their knowledge. You are what your teacher is, and if he knows a lot, you should be able to demonstrate this knowledge. ~ Yuchoku Higa

Seisan
section four

Step to the left with the right foot into an hourglass stance. The left arm sweeps outward through an outward block position. The right hand prepares for the palm block.

Execute a right palm block as the left hand scoops across the body beginning a circular motion.

Execute a left outward grab.

Raise the right hand in preparation for a hammer fist.

Seisan
Application Six

The attacker steps forward with the left foot and punches with the right hand. The defender executes a left outward grab and prepares the right hand for a hammer fist.

The defender executes a hammer fist to the attacker's temple.

More techniques can be extrapolated.
You can play with the right hand/ left hand attacks, dealing with secondary attacks, make an elbow roll/armbar with the hammer, use the left prep hand as a high block with multiple strike attacks, and so on.

The temple is supposed to be the thinnest part of the skull. Still, the skull is built to take impact, so practice your brick breaking until you have enough power to break a skull.

Execute a right hammer fist to the left palm.

The second figure is the view from the rear.

Almost as if you are bouncing the fist off the palm circle/scoop the right hand across the body as you executes a left palm block.

Execute a right outward grab.

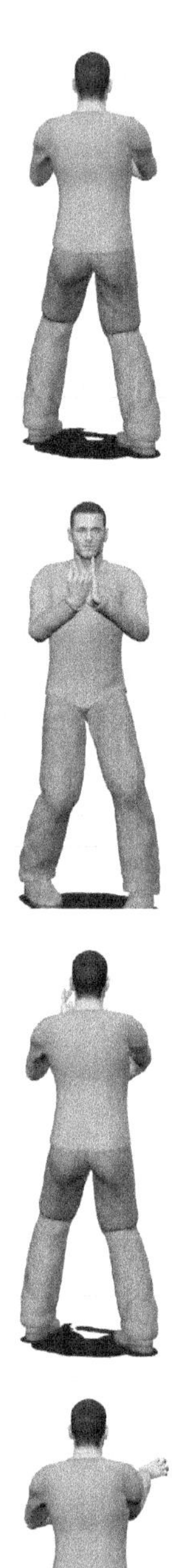

Seisan
Application Seven

This is an easy one.

The attacker punches with the left hand. The defender steps back with the left foot as he catches the attacker's left hand with his left hand. The defender then uses the hammer fist to the attacker's left elbow. This can be a break, an arm bar, an elbow roll, or even the start of an entry to a split.

This technique can be built into an arm pounding drill very easily. It is a virtual duplicate of motion used in some of the escrima or silat drills. Catch the arm, pound the arm, take turns striking/pounding.

I am a fan of arm toughening drills. Unfortunately, I have seen them work to the point of disfigurement. Thunderbolt Chow is said to have trained one of his hands so much it was so ugly he always kept it in his pocket.

I know of young man who pounded on a telephone pole to toughen his fist. He ended up with disfigured knuckles that hurt when he punched things.

In the Kang Duk Won we did a simple 'eight step blocking exercise,' developing low blocks and middle blocks on both sides of the arms.

If you do the forms properly, with grounding and breathing and so on, you will learn to focus first your muscles, then your energy, into your strike, or the part of your body being struck.

Execute a left palm strike.

The palm strike is interesting in that it requires a wave like motion of the hand to achieve. The fingers point forward and the hand waves to a palm.

Chapter Thirty-Nine
Seisan
(section five)

In the past, it was expected that about three years were required to learn a single kata, and usually even an expert of considerable skill would only know three, or at most five, kata. ~ Gichin Funakoshi

Seisan
section five

Step to the rear and turn to the right into an hourglass stance. The right hand sweeps outward beginning a circle. The left hand sweeps inward.

The right hand scoops across the body and the left hand executes a palm block.

Execute a right outward grab.

Execute a left vertical fist strike.

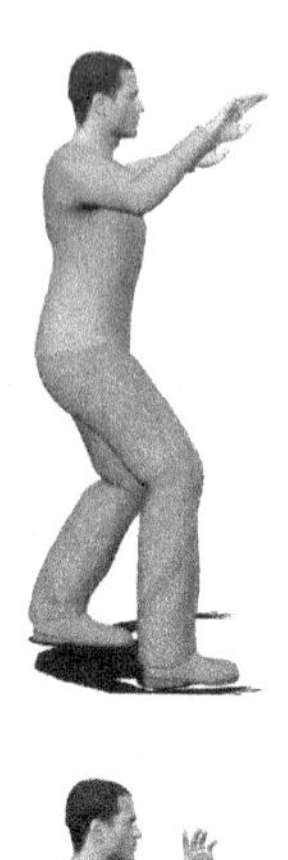

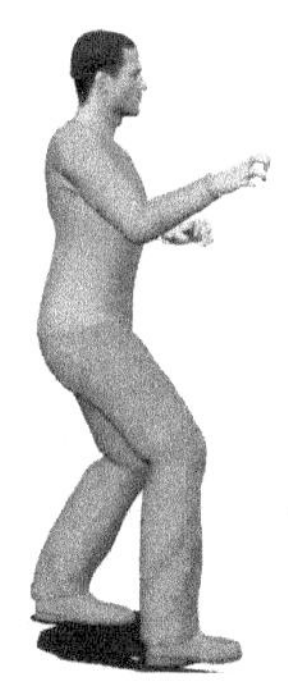

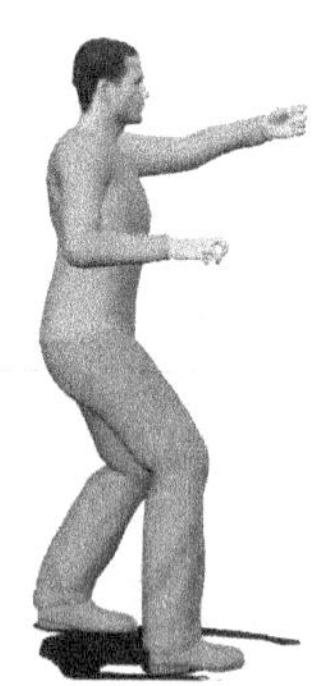

Chapter Forty
Seisan
(section six)

It is necessary to drink alcohol and pursue other fun human activities. The art (Karate) of someone who is too serious has no flavor. ~ Choki Motobu

Seisan
section six

Step to the left with the right foot into an hourglass stance facing to the rear. The left hand sweeps outward and the right hand sweeps inward.

The left hand scoops across the body as the right hand executes a palm block.

Execute a left outward grab.

Execute a left snapping/locking kick.

It snaps, but uses the hips and locks momentarily. The hips should both turn slightly and tilt slightly.

As you get familiar with this kick you can play with the timing. Do you turn and kick? Or turn as you kick? Or something else?

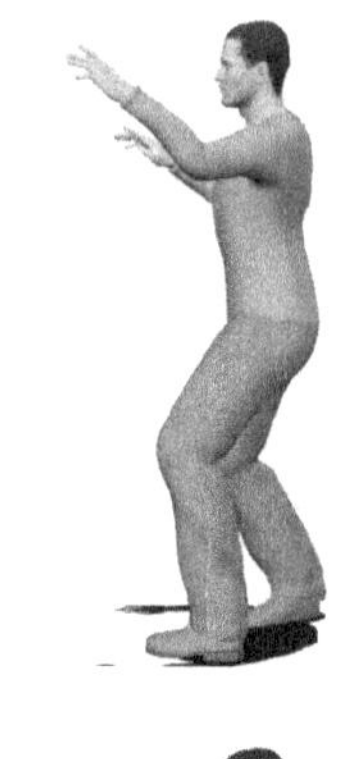

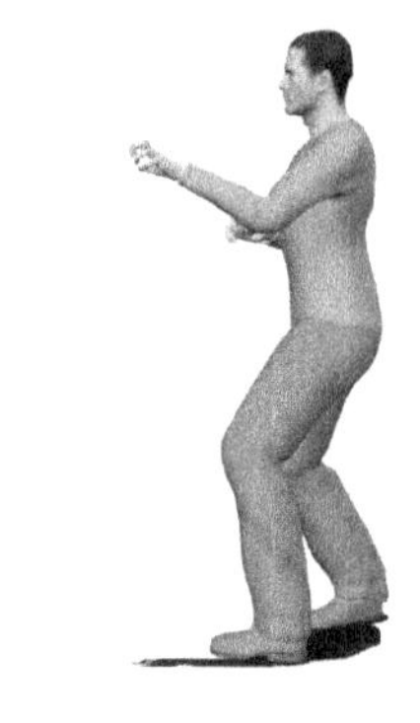

Seisan
Application Eight

The attacker punches and the defender executes a grab, or a slap/grab.

The defender can kick the groin, but if he doesn't want the opponent to get up, he should kick high on the thigh bone.

The top of the thigh bone has a ball on it. Kick that spot and the leg will fly back and your opponent will hit the ground. Kick hard enough and in the right spot and that bone can shear off. Your opponent will be down and screaming in pain.

I was teaching at a school and a rather chunky kid jumped out of a tree. He landed wrong and sheared the ball on top of his thigh bone off. He screamed, and couldn't stop. He then spent several months in the hospital. They couldn't just put a piece of metal in him like they do for most injuries and pop him back on his feet.

You should practice the front kick so it snaps, but locks for a moment. You have to thrust through the bone. The point is to have choice of whether you want to snap or thrust, and to have effectiveness with either method.

Set the left foot down in the hourglass stance then punch with the right hand towards the groin.

Execute a left punch to the belly button.

Execute a right punch to the chest.

Execute a left punch to the chin.

Execute double outward grabbing blocks.

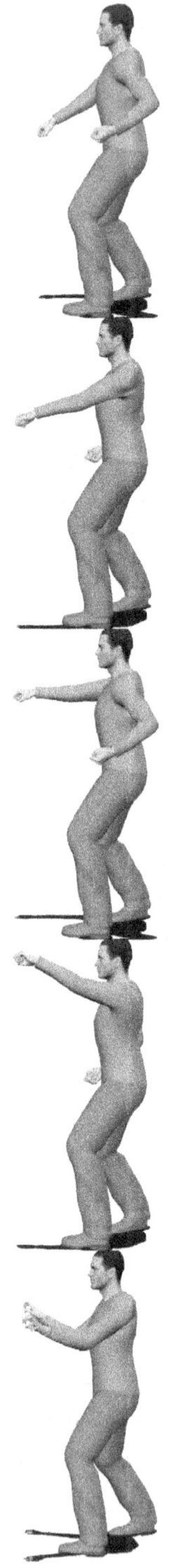

Seisan
Application Nine

This is the 'Override' drill.

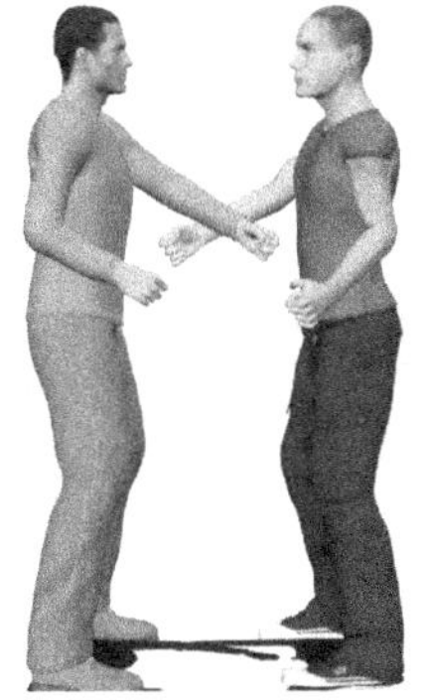

The partners face each other. Partner A on the left and partner B on the right.

Partner B strikes to the belly with the right hand. Partner A punches to the belly with his left hand, striking down across the top of Partner B's right wrist.

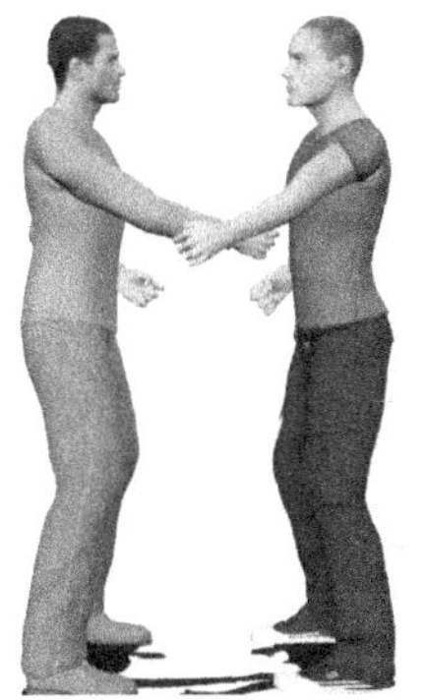

Partner B strikes to the belly with the left hand. Partner A punches to the belly with his right hand, striking down across the top of Partner B's left wrist.

Partner B strikes to the forehead with the right hand. Partner A punches to the forehead with his left hand, striking up across the bottom of Partner B's right wrist.

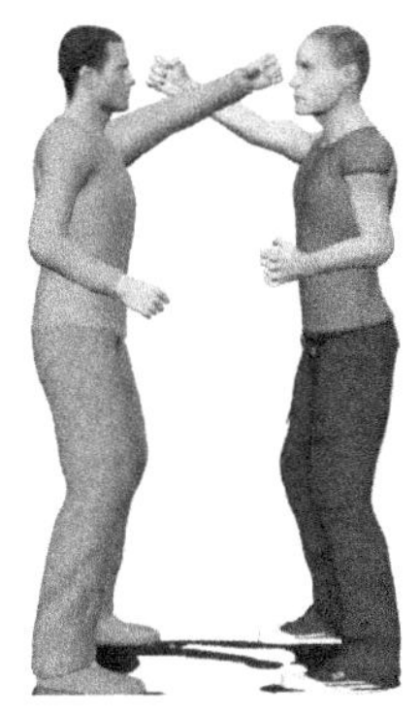

Partner B strikes to the forehead with the left hand. Partner A punches to the forehead with his right hand, striking up across the bottom of Partner B's left wrist.

It helps to have slight hip motion turning into each strike.

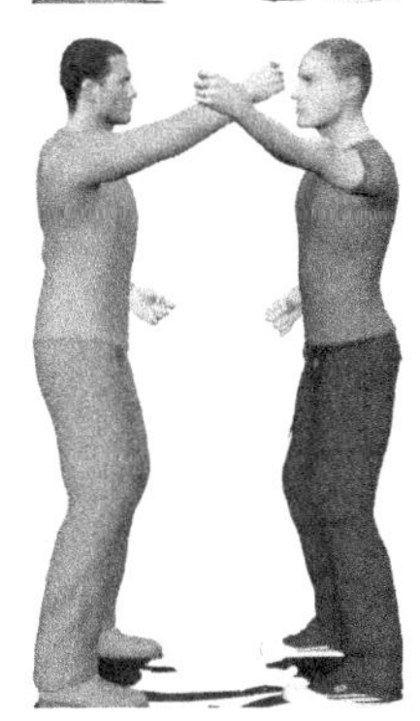

This is NOT a blocking drill. You are not blocking...you are punching through. You are 'overriding.'

I made this.

Step back with the right foot and turn 90 degrees to the right into an hourglass stance while holding the double outward grabbing blocks.

Circle the left hand up to a palm block and the right hand down to scoop across the body.

Execute a right outward grabbing block.

Execute a left vertical fist.

Retract the left fist to the double outward grabbing position.

Chapter Forty-One
Seisan
(section seven)

Karate does not have any one style. Karate molds an individual to be the only object of defense or offense and, through this, it teaches the fundamental concept of self-protection. ~ Kanken Toyama

Seisan
section seven

Step with the right foot to the left in front of the left foot and turn 180 degrees into an hourglass stance. The left hand sweeps out and the right hand sweeps in.

Circle the hands to execute a right palm block.

Execute a left outward grabbing block.

Execute a right vertical fist.

Chapter Forty-Two
Seisan
(section eight)

Spirit first, technique second. ~ Gichin Funakoshi

Seisan
section eight

Take a half moon step forward with the right foot as you sweep the right hand down in an inverted low (guiding) block.

Continue the circling of the hand to a right outward grab.

Execute a left vertical fist.

Take a half moon step forward with the left foot as you sweep the left hand down in an inverted low (guiding) block.

Seisan
Application Ten

This is in the form, but it is also in the matrixing of techniques form this form.

The attacker kicks with the left foot. The defender steps back with the right foot and slaps (guides) the foot outward.

The attacker sets forward. He is usually off balance because of being guided outward, so he will not strike with the left hand, but the right, which is more in position for the follow up.

The defender executes a grab, or a slap grab if the attacker launches two punches.

The defender pulls the attacker's arm and executes a strike to the chest.

Obviously, you can lift the leg for a throw, or dig the fingers into the biceps and take the attacker down that way.

By studying the matrixing of strikes and blocks you become able to accurately and always predict exactly what the opponent is doing, and right in the middle of action. But remember. 'It takes work to make it work.'

Complete the half moon step into an hourglass stance as you execute a left outward grabbing block.

Execute a right vertical fist.

Step back with the right foot as you protect the face with a left palm and the groin with a right inward palm.

Bring the left foot up in a crane stance as you turn sideways and execute a left hooking low block and a right high block.

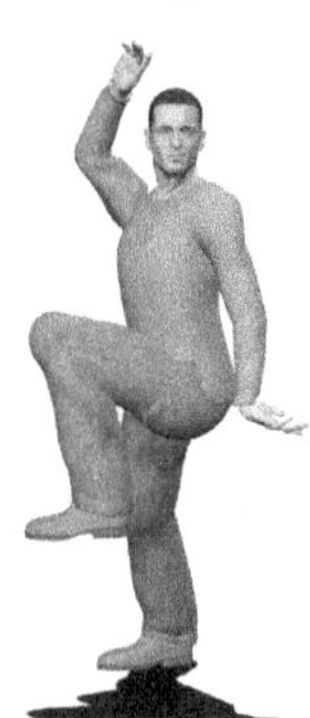

Seisan
Application Eleven

This is a variation of the perfect technique, which is firmly rooted in the matrix of strikes and blocks. Remember that this technique can be used for either foot, either hand or combination of hands, or side of the body for splitting.

The attacker kicks, the defender moves back into a crane stance (he could side kick the attacker's leg if he wishes) as he executes a right high block and catches the attacker's foot with a low hooking block.

The defender sets down and strikes. The defender moves forward, slapping the strike to the side.

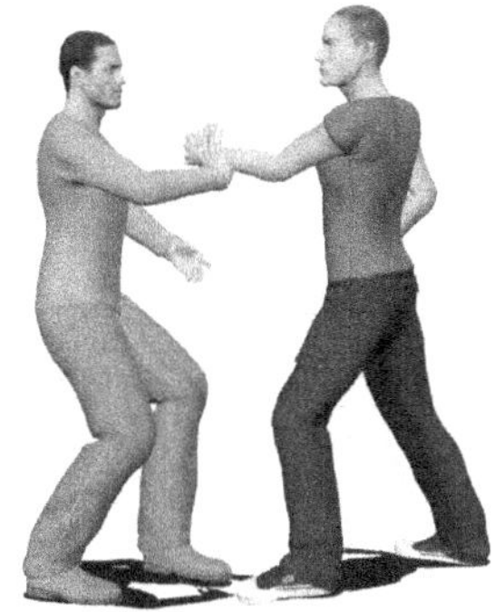

The attacker throws another strike, and the attacker takes another step into a horse stance as he grabs it with an outward grabbing block.

Please note that this technique is going through a collapsing of distances, which aligns with the 'kick/punch/knee/elbow matrix.

The technique is continued on the following right hand page.

Step forward with the left foot as you cover the face with the right palm block.

Step forward with the right foot as you execute a left outward grabbing block.

Sink into a horse stance as you execute a right elbow to the left hand.

Bring the right hand over to slap downward. The hands will do a vertical circle in this sequence.

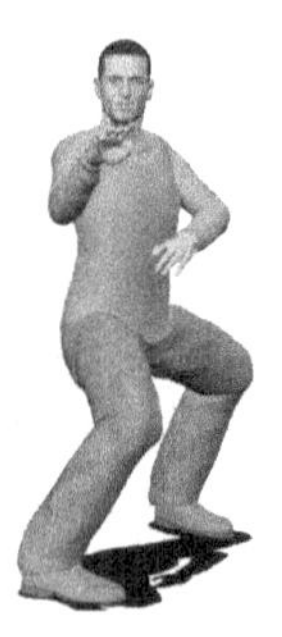

The defender shuffles in as he executes a right elbow strike to the chest. If needed, the defender can add an elbow spike to the chest.

The defender extends the right hand and, if necessary, shuffles forward to split the attacker.

Note that the defender's right knee points inward to disrupt the attacker's stance.

There are *many* techniques which can be extrapolated form this move.

Continue the circle of the hands

Execute a right horizontal fist.

Return to the beginning stance.

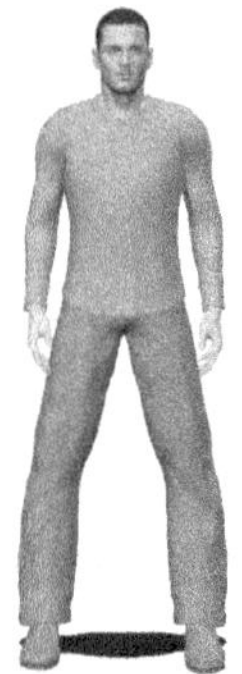

Chapter Forty-Three
Iron Horse
(section one)

Karate may be referred to as the conflict within yourself, or a life-long marathon which can be won only through self-discipline, hard training, and your own creative efforts. ~ Shoshin Nagamine

Below is the bonus video for the Iron Horse.

iron horse front.mp4   https://youtu.be/_McLjx129o0

The Iron Horse
section one

All movements are side to side in a horse stance in this form.

Stand with the feet together, hands in front of the groin.

Cross step to the right with the left foot.

Step into a horse stance as you execute a right outward middle block with open hand.

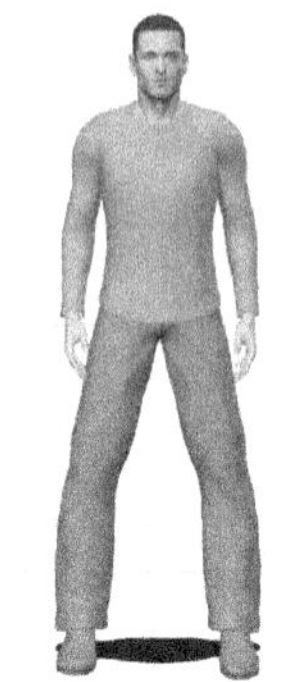

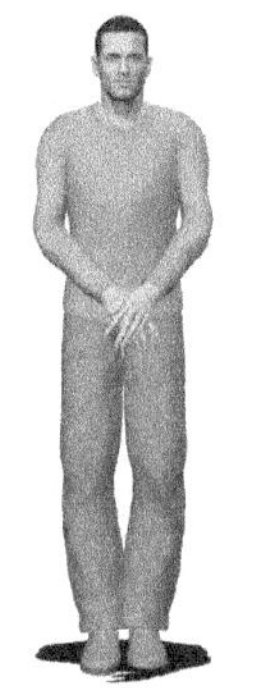

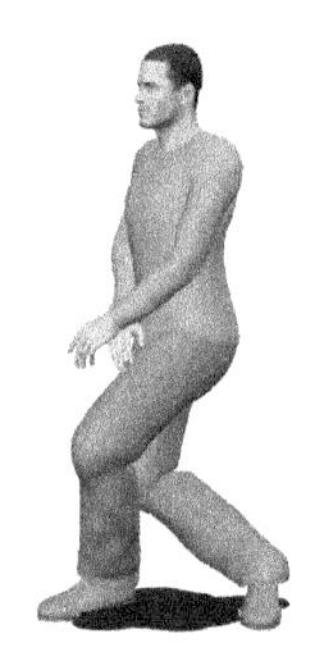

The Techniques of the Horse Form

I don't show techniques for this form. I used to, but I realized, especially after people started learning matrixing, that their progress was such that they had outgrown the need for specialized techniques.

Instead of checking to see if a person understood a form, which has already been done on seven forms, I was interested in whether they could create techniques from a form.

Could they see a motion and understand the self defense potential in it?

When you study Karate, even though I have made it a science with matrixing, you are studying an art. What is it that elevates art above all else?

Imagination.

Not memorization, though that is necessary in the beginning.

Not discipline, though that is crucial to learning control, which is essential to the fact of art.

The secret of art is imagination. So instead of turning out fellows with lighting reflexes who could knock the apples off a bull, I was interested in whether I had created an artist.

An artist will be able to create a situation where he never has to knock the apples off a bull.

Imagination. It is what makes you a human being. That is the secret of the art.

Twist the top half of the body to the right and strike the right palm with the left elbow.

Lower the right hand, palm down, and execute a left vertical backfist.

Untwist the top half of the body and look to the left, The right hand should be chambered and the left hand across the body with the fist palm down.

Execute a left low block to the left.

Doing the Complete Form

Kima Chodan, or Tekki One, or The Iron Horse, is the only complete form in Karate. Every other form is only a half form, or a form done on only one side.

I find it interesting that people who have studied karate, and the forms of karate, for years, decades, think they have studied the whole art.

This form has both the right side and the left side of the form in its entirety. Pinan one thru Pinan five only do the form on one side. And how many karateka take the time to do the form on the opposite side?

Sure, there is a symmetry to the forms, but that is not the same as doing the forms on both sides. I tell people they have to do the form on both sides.

I don't do this because a person has to be equally powerful on each side.

I do this because the person's mind must not become rigid. A person who takes these forms and does them on one side has limited himself. His mind is not able to take geometric forms in motion and see them on both sides in his head. By doing the forms on both sides his head 'loosens up.' He becomes more able to visualize the forms.

That is the point here, not to train people on both sides equally, but to make their heads able to visualize motion, to warp it, to shift, to turn it inside out. This is crucial to seeing and understanding the geometry an attacker might use.

I also used to make people do their forms backwards, or while holding weapons, and so on.

Twist the upper half of the body to the left as you execute a right punch to the left.

Step across the left foot and to the left with the right foot. (I usually do the punch as I step.)

Take another step and pivot to the right in a horse stance as you execute a right outward middle block.

Execute a right low block and a left outward middle block.

Horse Meditation

We would do something called 'Kima Chasie,' which meant 'Horse Meditation.' It is a very common drill. One simply sits in the horse stance, a high block with one hand, and extends a beak, fingers to the rear, with the other hand. Just focus on the finger tips. and breath. Simple and dimple.

Pretty much everybody hated this drill. Nobody liked to sit in a deep horse stance for any period of time. It hurts the legs, you know?

But I heard people talk about being able to stand in it for a half hour, and how it gave them mystical powers, yadda yadda.

Well, yeah. That's what I'm all about, right?

So I practiced for a few months, and then decided to blow it all out. I was going to beat this stupid exercise. (I didn't think of it as meditation).

I thought about it a lot, and I decided that I wasn't going to let the pain beat me. My precise thought was that 'it's only pain. It's not going to kill me.'

So I started. A minute passed. It hurt, but…so what. I wasn't going to die.

Another minute. And not to speak French, but it friggin' hurt! But, I toughened up inside. It was only pain. It wasn't going to kill me.

Another minute and…I popped right out of my head. I was existing as a floating mote of awareness about a foot above and sort of behind my head.

I was no longer a fleshy, meaty kind of body. I was a ghost, an awareness, I could look in all directions without the need for eyeballs.

So I stayed there for a while. No pain, no hurry, no need to be or do anything. But when I tried to move my body, to assert control over my flesh, I couldn't move. I lurched and I tugged, and I finally just tried to unbalance myself enough to start motion.

I fell right, smack, square on my face, but that didn't really hurt. The idea of falling on my face hurt more.

Bring the right hand up to the front as if grabbing a shirt front as you prepare the left hand for striking.

Bring the right hand back across the body as you execute a left inward middle block.

Very quickly, bring the left foot up, as if the sole is blocking a kick.

Before you can fall replace the left foot in the horse stance as you execute a left palm down outward middle block to the left.

The Sole Block

I used two exercises to improve my Sole Block.

First, as in the top figure right, I put one hand down and practiced slapping my right palm with my left sole.

Second, I placed one hand against a wall and held my foot with the other hand in a 'static' stance.

This second exercise enlightened me. Almost immediately I understood how to create a line of energy from my foot through my body to my hand.

This led me to immediately re-evaluate every posture I knew.

I treated this like Horse Mediation, focusing on my breathing and just ignoring the pain.

Before I did this exercise my sole block was sort of worthless. After I did it I found that it was easy to just slap kicks away with the sole of my foot.

Very quickly bring the right foot upward in a sole block.

Replace the right foot in a horse stance as you execute a right downward block.

Look to the left as you bring the right hand to the chamber position and hold the left arm across the body.

Twist the upper body to the left as you execute execute double punches to the to the left.

Chapter Forty-Four
Iron Horse
(section two)

A punch should stay like a treasure in the sleeve. It should not be used indiscriminately." – Chotoku Kyan

The Iron Horse
section two

Execute a left outward middle block with the palm facing upward.

Twist the upper body to the left as you execute a right elbow strike to the left palm.

Lower the left hand as you execute a right vertical back fist.

Untwist the upper body and look to the right. The left hand should be in the chamber position and the right hand should be across the body with the fist palm down.

Meditation

Meditation is one of the most misunderstood things in the world, in the martial arts, and even in the fields that practice meditation. Simply, they can't effectively define it.

The human being has only two directions to look in. Outward at the world, or inward to the self. Whichever direction you look in requires discipline to focus the attention.

An easy method of meditation is to focus on something to the exclusion of the rest of the world. Look at the flame of a candle and ignore the world.

The point of meditation is to focus on the world and eliminate distractive thoughts; to virtually erase the mind's existence in the scheme of things.

Sit with your back a tree and listen to the world, and *don't have any thoughts.*

That's meditation, when you have no thoughts, but simply exist.

If you've been there and done that you will realize something interesting: the world is a very fun and interesting place.

When you do the form, and think only about the form, with no distraction, allowing no distraction, then you are meditating. Over just the course of a few work outs you will find yourself a different person. Over a couple of years and you will find that it's sort of distracting to be around people who don't have this peace of mind.

Execute a right low block to the right.

Twist the upper half of the body to the right as you execute a left punch to the right.

Step across the right foot and to the right with the left foot (I always punch as I step).

Take another step and pivot to the right in a horse stance as you execute a right outward middle block.

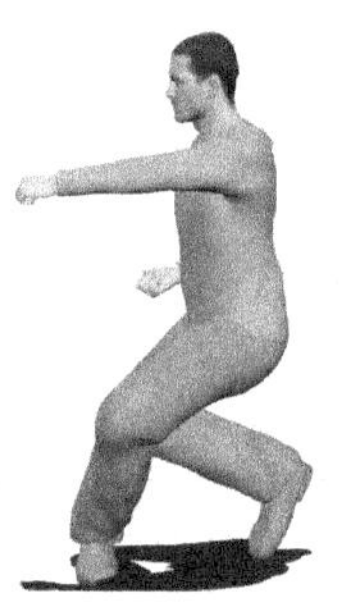

Meditation Again

Karate is meditation. Every time you spend a minute focusing on only one thing, that is a minute closer to yourself. Every form is a prayer, and the more you pray the more exalted you become.

Once you have committed the form to intuition your prayer becomes multi faceted. Hold your form motionless and discover a world of motion. Do your form intensely enough and you discover the world is motionless.

Here's the key to understanding this: you are playing soccer, focusing on the player running with you. As you run you realize that you and he have created a world between yourselves, and the rest of the world is sliding off your reality.

And, the last thing on this thing of meditation. I read a book by Talbot Mundy, fiction, wherein the statement was made: *If you can concentrate on one thing for three minutes you will rule the world.*

I found this interesting, and decided to do it. I was in a parking lot on lunch break at the time, sitting on the curb waiting for lunch to end.

I picked up a rock. A commonplace piece of stone. No different from any other piece of stone in the world, at least to my honed senses. I placed the stone on the ground and stared at it.

One minute. I was a roaring tiger, determined to conquer the universe.

Two minutes. I was doing it…sure was taking a long time, though.

Three minutes. Damn, this is boring. I stood up and went back to work.

I had taken maybe three steps when I realized, like a bolt out of the blue, the secret of the universe. The rock wasn't boring. It was me. I was the one who created my experience, and if I thought the rock was boring, I was creating boredom.

Since that experience I have *never* been bored. Even just sitting still has become an exciting activity.

Execute a left low block and a right outward middle block.

Bring the left hand up to the front as if grabbing a shirt front as you prepare the right hand for striking.

Bring the left hand back across the body as you execute a right inward middle block.

Very quickly, bring the right foot up, as if the sole is blocking a kick.

Changes I Made to the Iron Horse

I never stand with my feet together. That is unbalanced and defeats the idea of being able to move in any direction (sideways in this instance) quickly without pre-motion.

I don't punch both hands to the side at the end of the form. I do a punch and a high block. This feeds the next move wonderfully.

There is one move that causes pain to my left knee. I take it easy on that move. It's not the form, it's my body, or it would hurt my other knee on the other side of the form.

I cogitate as to whether placing the hand one over the other at the beginning of the form would be better as a crossed wrist low block.

When I punch across my form prior to stepping in the direction of the form I slur those moves together so that I am not twisting my upper body, but thrusting myself in a direction with the force of my punch.

I don't consider certain blocks as outward blocks, but as uppercuts.

I consider the reaching forward, after the simultaneous low block and outward middle block, as a grab to the shirt front so I can break their nose. This has a tendency to teach me how to ground while I am facing somebody in a face on wide stance. This helps me learn to ground and yet use power.

For a form with limited technique I consider it one of the strongest forms in all Karate.

I thought the form was for fighting while on the back of a horse. My instructor told me it was for fighting sideways in rice paddies. The real reason is likely that the creator thought it created energy specific to the horse stance.

Before you can fall replace the right foot in the horse stance as you execute a right palm down outward middle block to the left.

Very quickly bring the left foot upward in a sole block.

Replace the left foot in a horse stance as you execute a left downward block.

Look to the right as you bring the left hand to the chamber position and hold the right arm across the body.

Fighting

In a short while we will be getting into freestyle methods.

I fought and went to tournaments when I was studying Kenpo. I was an instructor and though I was deadly. Then I went to the Kang Duk Won and got my ass handed to me.

For two years I wasn't allowed to freestyle. I only did freestyle drills. Fight with the left side, fight with the feet only. Fight with the arms only. Fight using only inward and outward blocks. Do strikes with the back of the hand only to the hips or shoulders. And so on.

When I was finally given the green light to do open. Freestyle I was stunned. Freestyle was no longer a fight, it was scientific assessment and dismemberment.

And I kicked ass.

But I also became a more gentle person.

Doing these drills made me look, and when I had looked enough I couldn't be fooled.

After this, when I did freestyle with people from other schools they would become discouraged very quickly. I had no openings, I knew what they were going to do before they did it.

In short, I wasn't playing the game of freestyle anymore. I was scientifically assessing and dismembering.

Because I did the applications I knew how to dismember the body. Because I had done freestyle drills (instead of playing tag) I was able to look at an opponent and understand what he was doing.

Why don't people like this anymore? Why don't they teach the real art? Because children want to play tag and don't want to learn. And teachers let them get away with this.

Twist the upper body to the left as you execute execute double punches to the to the left.

Retract the right foot to the natural stance.

Chapter Forty-Five
Advanced Matrixing in Karate

The techniques of kata have their limits and were never intended to be used against an opponent in an arena or on a battlefield. ~ Choki Motobu

Below are the bonus videos for the full forms

Full pinan.mp4   https://youtu.be/wSdKbjsrbPk

Full sanchin.mp4   https://youtu.be/j9SKNvqwkD8

Full seisan.mp4   https://youtu.be/YOLxUiuOZE4

Matrixing Step by Step

When I began learning different martial arts I would make long lists of forms and techniques. I would try combining arts and end up with super long lists. I would create new arts, and the super long lists became even longer. I would try to make one art that encompassed all arts, and the lists were too long to write down. I mean…*thousands* of techniques. To get around this road block of having too many techniques to list, I started using a matrix.

Matrixing, to describe it briefly, while it has many little 'tricks,' utilizes something called a 'truth table.' Truth tables come from Boolean Algebra, and are, I believe, used to describe three dimensional figures on two dimensional surfaces. Prime examples of the usefulness of this algebra would be TVs and computer screens.

An example of a truth table would be:

	plus	minus
plus	plus/plus	plus/minus
minus	minus/plus	minus/minus

You can see that this table offers every possible combination of pluses and minuses.

Plus
Minus
Plus/Plus
Plus/Minus
Minus/Plus
Minus/Minus

To apply this to the martial arts let's consider the Kebons, or Taikyokus. Here is a matrix for the original four blocks. It is a simple list which virtually every school has.

	Low	High	Out	In

The list makes sense (block in all four directions, up, down, side and side), but students are sometimes left on these basics for six months to a year before they get a Pinan (Heian). And when they are taught Pinan One consider the following Matrix

	low	high	rolling hammers	knife block

This is not a matrix, but another list, and the student is taught two basics, which he has already learned, a weird combination, and an advanced basic block (knife hand).

To understand the significance of this ask yourself why so many students drop out. Because they are on the runway too long.

Yes, they do learn other stuff, and it is all important, but now consider the real matrix, the one the student learns in the first month of training in my system.

	low	high	out	in
low	low/low	low/high	low/out	low/in
high	high/low	high/high	high/out	high/in
out	out/low	out/high	out/out	out/in
in	in/low	in/high	in/out	in/in

This is the matrix of blocks for the first four blocks (hi, low, out and in). But it is not a list so much as a graph which covers the four basics and every combination of the four basics.

The real glory here is that nothing is skipped over, there are no 'blank spots.' And what are blank spots?

What if you learned, as your basics, Low, High and Outward?

The student learns the three basics, and is defending himself in three directions, but has to turn his body to the other side to block in the fourth direction. This isn't totally logical, but he wasn't taught the fourth block. the result is that he is confused because the set up doesn't make sense.

It would be the same as teaching a person to count but leaving out the number five. The student knows there should be another number because he has one more finger than numbers, but...it just doesn't make sense, and he gets frustrated, and he thinks that math is only for idiots, it's some kind of voodoo for ignorant people.

This is what happens in the martial arts.

Past the basics a student learns a sweep, but might not be taught how a sweep works with a low block, a high block, an outward block, and inward block. So he neglects sweeps because they don't make much sense, and… his art now has blank spots.

And when you start combining arts to try to fill the blank spots you run into other problems. Techniques are redundant, done with emphasis on different mechanics, are at odds with conflicting concepts, and so on

So a person is given a list of techniques, and he is going down the list, and he comes to a blank spot. At that point he is distracted by *what isn't there!* His mind stops, and he wonders, and he keeps looking at the blank spot, wondering what is supposed to be there, and his education breaks down at that point. And even if he manages to keep going, there is a blank spot in his mind.

And the poor instructor, doing his best, is stumped because he can't see what isn't there because…*it isn't there!*

The conclusion is this: Past the basics most arts are conglomerations of techniques that some fellow thought were useful, that fulfilled some concept in his head. This haphazard approach results in lots of blank spots, or techniques that were taught without thought of what techniques should go between one technique and the next.

A simple matrix reveals these blank spots, and the education is automatically repaired. Beginning students learn faster, and advanced students suddenly achieve instant illumination concerning their art and the techniques thereof.

Here is the matrix for the *eight* basic blocks of karate.

You won't find any basics beyond this, and the 64 techniques that result from this matrix enable one to understand virtually everything there is in karate.

As you do this matrix you should consider what works and what doesn't work. Knowing what doesn't work is as important as knowing what does work.

You will have to explore the ranges of attacks, sweeps and resulting throws and locks and so on.

	low	high	out	in	x-low	x-hi	palm	inv lo
low								
high								
out								
in								
x-low								
x-hi								
palm								
inv lo								

Advanced Matrixing

In the first book of this duology I listed a number of techniques for Pinan Two. People can choose any number of techniques to practice, but for our purposes here let's say one has to learn ten techniques from the form. This is a good average number and easy to work with. You can choose more or less techniques as you wish.

If you start exploring your pinan two techniques with a matrix, using triangle or switch steps as needed, you will end up with a matrix, or list, of 100 techniques.

Doing these 100 techniques will give you more knowledge in what Pinan is and does than ten years of studying it doing just the ten techniques from which this matrix is drawn.

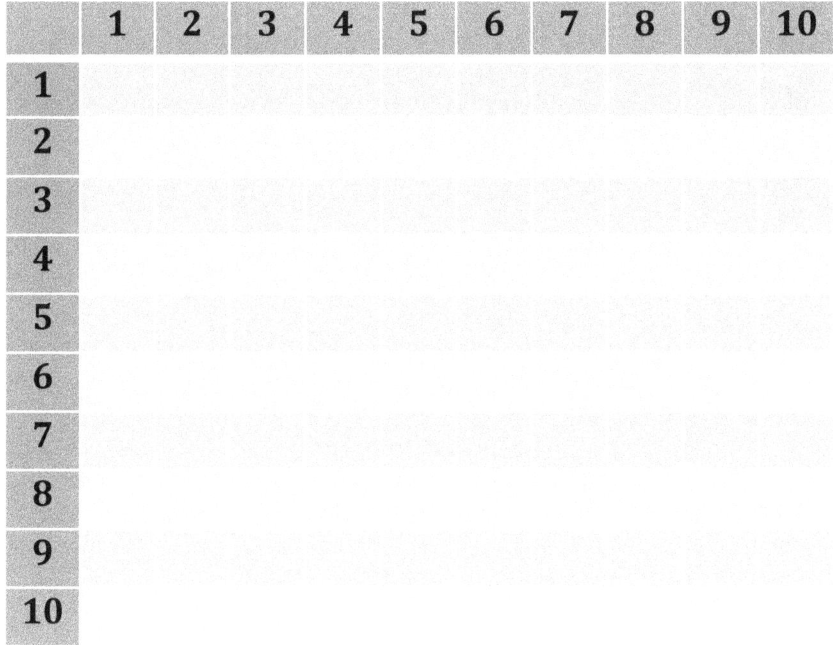

Doing all five pinans with matrixes like this you will have 500 techniques, and you will understand the pinans better than the person who made them up.

Matrix for Pinan One and Pinan Two

Once you have matrixed all five pinans with themselves you can start cross matrixing them. For instance, here's pinan one across the top and pinan two down the left column..

	1	2	3	4	5	6	7	8	9	10
1										
2										
3										
4										
5										
6										
7										
8										
9										
10										

You should also look at this matrix with pinan two across the top, and pinan one down the side.

You will now have another 100 techniques, which you will understand better than any 'master.' You will understand the different ways of entering techniques from other techniques (positions, situations, etc.) You will not be lost in mysticism and the search for mystical techniques.

Matrixes for All the Pinans

Here is a list of the possible matrixes.

pinan 1/pinan 1
pinan 1/pinan 2
pinan 1/pinan 3
pinan 1/pinan 4
pinan 1/pinan 5

pinan 2/pinan 1
pinan 2/pinan 2
pinan 2/pinan 3
pinan 2/pinan 4
pinan 2/pinan 5

pinan 3/pinan 1
pinan 3/pinan 2
pinan 3/pinan 3
pinan 3/pinan 4
pinan 3/pinan 5

pinan 4/pinan 1
pinan 4/pinan 2
pinan 4/pinan 3
pinan 4/pinan 4
pinan 4/pinan 5

pinan 5/pinan 1
pinan 5/pinan 2
pinan 5/pinan 3
pinan 5/pinan 4
pinan 5/pinan 5

Doing all these matrixes will fill in more blanks in your art than anybody in history has ever filled in. It will make you a better martial artist than anybody in history.

You will have done 2500 techniques and there will be virtually no blank spots.

And because you are not wasting your time learning out of order techniques and trying to get past blank spots you will become so familiar that you are intuitive, and the learning procedure will take one tenth the time.

You don't have to wallow in a glut of blank spots, simply do a matrix until you get it, then move on to the next matrix. You will be shocked at how fast people can learn this stuff.

If you spend a month or two on each matrix you will find that you will know everything in about 60 months. That's not a black belt in four or five years. That is absolute mastery.

But I don't ask you to believe me. Simply do a couple of matrixes and observe the changes in yourself, and how much you know and how polished you become.

I tell you, it is a whole new level of martial arts.

One thing that should be considered is that doing karate matrix style will allow for standardization of the material. Sure, there will always be stylistic differences, and there should be. It is an art, after all. But if students have slight disagreements simply ask if their technique works, and forget about stylistic differences.

Stylistic differences aside, Karate is a science, and we should avail ourselves of the logic inherent in science.

Thus, when you have gone through a few matrixes you will suddenly understand that you can, and should, use the matrixes for grading people.

The first eight belts are easy. If you decide to keep the eight levels of the lower belts you can simply have the person do the eight forms I have listed in this two book set.

For beyond black belt you simply divide the advanced matrixes I have just described through the belt levels.

This is the easiest path to acquire the complete knowledge of Karate. With NO politics. NO vested interests. NO domineering instructors. NO outside influences or distractions.

Suggested Training Methods

You must train in the forms every day. This will build your speed and strength. More important, it will build your energy and your awareness.

If you only work out with, say, weights, or at karate with only strength in mind, you will only build muscles.

If you work out at karate by looking at what you are doing, exploring potentials of motion, timing, different types of energy, you grow in awareness.

Which would you rather be? Strong or smart?

With that in mind I offer the following standard training methods. You should do them until they become a form of meditation. In this way you will grow awareness.

Pounding beans

There are many variations of this drill, but I prefer this one.

Simply get a sack (leather or canvas) of beans. Place the beans on a stool and drop your hand on it. Front hand, back hand, front hand, back hand.

Do not strike, just let the hand fall and try to 'feel,' to extend your awareness through the sack.

Makiwara

Cut a board until it is one inch thick at the top and two inches thick at the bottom. Bury it three feet deep, with a big stone in the bottom of the hole in front of the board, and a big stone a foot from the top of the hole but behind the board.

Fix a striking pad to the top and strike every day. I used to just tack two or three thicknesses of carpet samples to a tree. So you've got some leeway for creativity in this.

Don't strike with muscle, figure out how to extend the arm and just as it reaches full extension move your body weight into it.

I always say, 'full extension for full power,' for strikes.

1000 Sheets of Paper

I used to use a big, thick phone book for this, and I recommend this if you can find one.

No phone book to be had, however, simply glue one end of a ream of paper, let dry, and clamp it to a wall.

Practice striking the 1000 sheets daily. Use fingers, fists, chops, whatever. Try to not rip the paper…keep the impact in a straight line. Within six months your technique will be incredible.

Post Training

You can sink four posts in the ground and practice your forms on them, adapting your steps to the four posts.

I used to do this on cinder blocks on end, and I recommend this. If you make a mistake you will definitely learn to land with awareness.

Cardboard Training

I used to love doing this when I worked in a warehouse with lots of boxes. I would simply do techniques and try to leave little holes in the cardboard with my knuckles

The Mad Monkey Fist

Hold the hand two inches from a wall (wallboard).

Strike with the fingers. Do not bring the hand back, but fold the fingers and go forward to strike with the knuckles. Do not bring the hand back but make a fist and go forward to strike with the fist.

There are a lot of variations for this. I was particularly fond of striking with the middle finger, the index finger, the middle knuckle, the foreknuckle, then two punches of the fist. I would make a 'rhumba rhythm' while doing this.

I became pretty adept at this and could leave serious indentations in walls that I struck.

These drills will increase your strength, focus your mind, and help you create energy that can be channeled through your body and controlled in various other ways.

You should search for other methods, find what you really enjoy doing.

Do not think that you shouldn't do weight or other types of strength training. Just don't be locked into one method or another.

The most important thing is to do the drills daily. Set aside even 15 minutes, but preferably an hour, and just do the drills.

Do not think that just punching or kicking a bag will do anything. You must have objects that give way only a little, if you are going to understand what the universe is made of.

Do not work on just muscles. Work on relaxing, and breathing, and feeling the energy course through your body.

Anybody who degrades karate had never done these exercises, and certainly hasn't run into anybody who has done these exercises.

The Condition of Your Body

When you begin Karate your body is soft.

After doing karate your muscles don't become big and fat, they become dense.

I once had some deep tissue massage done for an injury I had incurred. The poor masseuse had a heck of a time. Even relaxed my muscles were hard as stone.

A year later I went back for a 'tune up,' and the masseuse told me he had finally found somebody with denser muscles than me. He had performed his massage on a marathon runner, and he said the muscles of his legs were that dense.

You don't want to be a big, bully boy. You want to be a mild fellow who slides through life without people's thoughts being altered by their impression of you.

I have played with weights, and with other forms of strength building, but I always returned to the body conditioning given through endless repetitions of forms.

Chapter Forty-Six
Freestyle

Karate is a lifetime study." — *Kenwa Mabuni*

Below is a bonus course, Dharma Combat,
which teaches my method of learning freestyle

Matrix Combat   http://churchofmartialarts.com/pss4mtrxcbot/

List of Freestyle Drills

Following is. a list of the freestyle drills I use in teaching. The order I put them in is adjustable, according to a student's abilities, experience, etc.

Done properly, these drills result in a fellow or gal who can fight using karate within a few hours.

One must not drown a person in these drills, but be knowledgeable as to which drill to apply when.

Freestyle, properly taught, is fun and easy. Really, it is a game of tag…just be sure to remember that it is a life and death game that you are preparing for.

Duck and Dodge
Rhythmic Freestyle
Rhythmic Freestyle (two strike)
Rhythmic Freestyle (One Way)
Flowstyle
Rolling Hands
Sticky Hands
Pushing Hands
Multiman

On the following pages I will give a brief description of the various methods.

You should know, before you start, that my method is not based on the human cockfight method of who can beat who. It is based on trust.

The most important thing I can tell you is that if somebody is getting beaten up all the time they won't want to study karate. You have to make sure that there is a give and take, especially in the beginning, so that students feel they are winning as much as they are losing.

Too much loss, or too much winning is bad.

The Alley

The Alley is the central strategy behind all freestyle. To understand it let's first realize that fighting is the idea of hitting (throwing) somebody without being hit (thrown).

The first rule of fighting is to control the distance. If you control the distance between you and your opponent you may control what weapons you will use, keeping to your strengths and his weaknesses

That brings us to The Alley.

Raise your hands so they are midway between high and low.

Place your hands so they are halfway between straight and bent.

Your hands should be pointing towards your opponent's shoulders.

If you widen your hands the opponent will punch down 'The Alley.'

If you move your hands closer together the opponent will punch around The Alley.

The opponent is now predictable, and with little practice your movements to block will become intuitive.

Duck and Block

You hold a stick, the opponent does not.

There are two commands: 'Duck' and 'Block.'

If you say 'Duck' you must swing the stick horizontally to the head, horizontally towards the feet, or vertically straight down on the head. The opponent may only bend the knees, jump, or step to the side. He may only step to the side in one direction, and the next time you swing downwards he must step sideways to his original y position.

If you say 'Block' you may only swing the stick diagonally and in such a manner that the opponent need only use low blocks or high blocks.

This is a wonderful drill to get the beginner to stop being scared and start looking at what is happening.

DO NOT overwhelm the student with speed. You should only go as fast as he can block or dodge. The point isn't for you to hit him, but to train him not to get hit. You would be shocked at how many supposedly high ranking belts don't understand this.

DO NOT strike hard with the stick, just touch.

Rhythmic Freestyle

I usually start students on this drill with short sticks.

One student strikes and the other student blocks.

The student who blocks now strikes, and the student who struck now blocks.

And they continue, back and forth.

The students may move about the mat taking ONLY one step when they block, and ONLY one step when they strike. And, yes, you will have to watch them for this constantly.

This is a downright magical drill. Done right a student learns to fight within minutes.

BUT…you have to make sure that they understand it is a slow motion drill.

DO NOT let the students overwhelm each other with speed. They should only go as fast as they can block or dodge.

Be aware, within two minutes the students will be trying to hit each other. This is because they watch too much TV, play too many video games, and are raised in a violent society.

The make or break point is when you get them to go slow and they begin to develop patience and understanding and begin to actually analyze motion.

Once the students can play with the sticks without fighting you can let them try it with punches and blocks.

You would be stunned at how many so called 'instructors' can't teach this drill. They are so obsessed with the 'hit 'em first' mentality that they can no longer think, let alone teach.

Two Strike Rhythmic Freestyle

This is a simple one: just have the first student strike twice in a row, and the other student block twice in a row.

Then the student who blocked strikes twice in a row, and the student who struck blocks twice in a row.

The student should ONLY take one step for each strike or block.

It is best to do this drill with sticks first, then progress to empty hands.

The interesting thing about this drill, is how little discussion is required. When a student turns his back, for instance, or does something else that is not protective of or advantageous to him, you simply tap him, or push him, or demonstrate how is exposed or out of position. You DON'T need to lecture. You DON'T need to use force. Just tap and grin, shove and smile, and he grins, and smiles, and he will be automatically self correcting within a short period of time.

If a student is having a rough time with this drill just move him back to the previous drill. If he's got it, but you think he needs a bit more polish, have him help others learn the drill. But don't let him talk and explain things. Make him touch and smile.

One Way Rhythmic Freestyle

You only spend a short time on the previous drills, just an hour or two over a week or two, then you introduce the student to One Way. This is a common drill with LOTS of benefits. I suggest that you do all drills with the student first before pairing him up with another, and watching them closely always.

One student steps forward and strikes and the other student steps back and blocks.

The same student keeps taking one step and striking, and the other student keeps stepping back and blocking, until the student blocking touches the wall (goes off the mat).

The students reverse roles, the blocker becomes the striker and the striker become the blocker, and they go the other way.

Here is where speed will start to pick up, and you can start to push the reality lightly.

Moving backwards gives the student time to analyze the motion.

Do not worry about backing up becoming a habit.

You can use sticks in this drill, then empty hands.

This drill can easily slide into freestyle. If the students are good that's good. But you have to watch and make sure the students are good, or that one isn't significantly better than the other. You don't need one student winning at the expense of the other.

Flowstyle

I usually do this with students who have learned enough grab arts and understand the basic theory of grab arts, that all you have to do is circle a joint to create a grab art.

The students simply take turns. One gets a wrist lock, then the other folds the elbow out, then the other one tried for a neck lock, and the other one tries for a sweep. And so.

You are not trying to do the whole lock to the floor or broken limbs.

You are taking the lock through the entry, then holding, even backing off if you have gone too far, so that your partner may effect his lock or throw.

Back and forth you go, it becomes fun and very educational.

Rolling Fists (Lop Sau)

I created this drill and it is the most advanced freestyle drill in history.

Other drills that are similar were usually limited, or slanted, and were good only for a slice of learning. But the Rolling Hands drill done correctly with all pieces is a complete art in itself.

There are six techniques in the beginning.

The jab (done as a backfist) which rolls over and over. The opponent catches the jab and rolls his own jab. You catch and roll your own jab, and back and forth we go.

The Front Hook. Instead of jabbing, swing the front arm around The Alley. The opponent blocks and punches with the other hand for the belly. The 'hooker' must block with a low inverted forearm and circle into The Jab.

The Rear Hook. Immediately after jabbing throw a hook with the rear hand. The opponent blocks and punches with the other hand for the belly. The 'hooker' must block with a low inverted forearm and circle into The Jab.

The Front Kick. Instead of jabbing, kick for the groin with the front foot. The opponent simply circles the hand and slaps the attacker's foot outward. The low slap rolls up to The Jab. Do not do a regular low block.

The Change. Instead of stopping the attacker's jab, the defender hooks it and pulls it in as he changes his stance and executes The Jab with the other side.

Change and Kick. Execute a change, then kick with the new front foot. The opponent must change with you then slap and roll the foot, or get kicked.

Once the student has the six pieces of the drill down you can look for split timing, throws, and so on. HOWEVER, you may think the student has the drill down prematurely if he can make all the blocks work. But he doesn't have the drill down until he can do Rolling Hands while generating the attacks. Sure, he might be able to defend, but he is always moving after the attack, responding to the attack. He must learn to generate the attack to be at cause.

The following illustrations are taken from the 'Nine Square Diagram' book.

1st Technique in Lop Sau
Rolling the Fist

Partners face each other at handshake distance, each with the same leg forward.

Partner A strikes with a front hand back fist to the face.

Partner B catches the back fist with his rear hand palm block.

When attacking move into a front stance and turn the waist along the plane of the feet.

When defending move into a back stance with the hips square to your opponent.

The back of the fist should slap into the palm like a ball into a glove.

The back fist simulates a jab.

2nd Technique in Lop Sau
Front Hand Hook Punch

Instead of striking with a back fist, partner A strikes with a front hand hook to the face.

Partner B executes a back hand high block.

Partner B punches to the mid-section with the front hand.

Partner A utilizes a 'dangling forearm' block.

Partner A rolls back into the circling fist of the first technique.

The drill is based on the constant circling of the fists. Any deviation is followed by a return to the circling motion of the back fist.

3rd Technique in Lop Sau
Rear Hand Hook Punch

After the first technique is executed, Partner A doesn't move back, but rather executes a rear hand hook to the face.

Partner B executes a front hand high block.

Partner B punches to the mid-section with the rear hand.

Partner A executes a front hand 'dangling forearm' block.

Partner A continues the circle of the dangling forearm into the first technique of the drill.

4th Technique in Lop Sau
Slapping the Front Kick

Instead of striking with the initial back fist, Partner B executes a kick to the groin area.

Partner A slaps the ankle outward with the front hand.

Partner A circles the slap into the circling of the hands.

You begin training this drill slowly, adding pieces slowly, and the speed of the blocks and strikes begins to increase.

In a very short time, maybe an hour or two, the partners are moving with blinding speed and never miss a block.

5th Technique in Lop Sau
Changing Sides

Instead of catching the back fist, partner A hooks the inside of partner B's arm and pulls. He should be stepping back with the front foot as he pulls, but only to the depth of his rear foot.

Partner A steps forward with the back foot and strikes with the new front hand.

If partner B has picked up on the change, and changed with the attack, he will catch the back fist with his other palm.

If partner B doesn't change a big hole in his defense opens up and Partner A will touch Partner B on the face with his back fist.

It will become apparent quickly that if either partner misses a block, is late, or deviates from the pattern, a hole in his defenses will result.

6th Technique in Lop Sau
Changing with a Kick

As in the last technique Partner A executes a hooking pull with his front hand as he changes. Instead of striking with a backfist, however, he will execute a kick with his new front leg.

Partner B should change with partner A and slap the attacking foot on the inside ankle with his new front hand.

Partner B should return to the first technique of the drill.

Sticky Hands

Sticky Hands, or 'Chi Sao,' is practiced in many arts, but predominately in Wing Chun Kung Fu.

This drill is best described by a teacher, or at least must be augmented with some good video.

The main thrust of the drill is to twine the hands and move them in circular patterns.

The essence of the drill is not to resist, but to give way. This is the opposite of most martial arts, and demonstrates this author's opinion that to fully understand the hard one must understand the soft.

I advise you to seek out good instruction, and apply the principles in this book to the drill.

Pushing Hands

Another drill that is practiced in many arts, but predominately in Tai Chi Chuan.

Like the Sticky Hands drill, this drill teaches one to empty the body. Not just the hands, but the whole body. Not to resist force, but to go with it. It is a phenomenal drill that totally changes the way a hard martial artist thinks.

You haven't lived until you've been tossed around like a rag doll by an accomplished practitioner of Push Hands.

Like Sticky Hands, this drill is best described by a teacher, or at least must be augmented with some good video.

Multiman Freestyle

While Sticky Hands empties the arms in non-resistance, and Pushing Hands empties the body, multiman freestyle empties the body…in motion.

It is practiced mostly in Aikido and results in wonderful throws and locks.

Other arts do play with it, but they tend to include portions of impact focused arts.

While reality is good, one should always seek out the purest form before altering it for reality. One must search for the concepts if one wishes to understand the purity of a theory.

Advanced Theories of Freestyle

I have covered the methods I use when training people.

I usually focus the most on Lop Sau, then Push Hands. Sticky Hands is useful, but I find that Lop Sau and Push Hands work best for me.

In the past I used many different types of drills.

These included the drill from the Kang Duk Won called 'Hi lo.' This was a simple back and forth, striking the hips or the shoulder with the back of the palm, and using different types of blocks to defend.

I don't use hi-lo for two reasons. One, people are fragile now and they don't like the pain. Oddly, this wasn't even one of the painful drills. Two, Lop Sau works ten times better than anything I've ever seen.

Another drill was 'In out.' This was a simple punch either down the center, or a hook, and the student had to figure out whether he should close the alley with an inward block, or open the alley with an outward block.

This is a very useful drill. I do use it, and even hi-lo, in specific instances. As I get better and better at teaching Lop Sau, however, I find less and less need to use those drills.

You'll notice that these 'advanced theories' revolve around basics. That's because the secret of good martial arts is good basics. There is no other way, there is no substitute.

The main thing I do, when teaching freestyle is to go into three specific theories.

One, present the hands by pointing them to the shoulders. Make an alley, then guide the opponent into striking straight so you can close the alley and trap him, or guide him into hooking so you can block hard and set him up for your on strikes.

Two, the body should be wedge on to the opponent; it should never be presented with the body 'flat,' or facing the opponent. The point here is that you should present only weapons to your opponent, and never targets. Once a person understands how rigid a rule this is it becomes easy to set yourself up as if opening a target and luring an opponent into a bad strike.

Three, I tell people that they should avoid 'crossing the centerline.' This means that you don't put the right hand over the left part of the body, or the left hand over the right part of the body. This is sometimes a subtle concept, but it is fantastic once understood and applied to freestyle.

The most important thing to remember, when you are teaching somebody how to fight is that you must emphasize trust.

Sure, you can do something they don't know and strike them, but they learn nothing, and they start not trusting you.

Instead, go slow. Take your time. If you do something the student doesn't understand then you must stop, break it down and let them do it, otherwise they will stop trusting you.

People who don't trust you will not accept information from you.

Heck, why would somebody want to learn from somebody who keeps beating them up?

When the person has learned sufficiently that he understands the game, then you can begin playing seriously, but…remember: Karate is a science. Teach my way and there will be constant progress. Teach any other way and progress is two steps back for three steps forward.

THE LAST WORD

You can apply the material of this book, the concept of matrixing, to any martial art you study.

You can apply matrixing to any field of knowledge.

You may begin your study of matrixing, and the martial arts taught by Al Case, at:

MonsterMartialArts.com

Have you read…

All martial arts boiled down to nine simple forms…nine simple techniques.

This art can be done with the explosiveness of Karate, the meditative quality of Tai Chi, the linking of Pa Kua Chang.

Techniques are applicable on the mat, on the street, or in the ring.

This is the last martial arts book you will ever need!

Have you read…

Unique Tai Chi Chuan concepts change karate drastically.

Age old truths about karate and the martial arts will be obvious.

Techniques hidden by 'Masters' will be revealed.

'Chi power' of Tai Chi Chuan will grow through karate forms.

A different way of looking at both Karate and Tai Chi Chuan.

Have you read…

Five complete arts, including forms, two man forms, training drills, techniques, freestyle methods. The five arts are:

Matrix Karate
Shaolin Butterfly
Butterfly Pa Kua Chang
Matrix Tai Chi Chuan
Monkey Boxing

Have you read...

Matrixing is the most important development of the martial arts in history.

This volume holds three books written by the 'inventor' of Matrixing, Al Case.

These three books are NOT books of technique and form, but are directly concerned with the logic and theory of matrixing.

They are:

Martial Arts 101: Fixing the Martial Arts
The Science of Matrixing in the Martial Arts
Binary Matrixing in the Martial Arts

Have you read…

Behind the Martial Arts there is a philosophy, it is called Neutronics. This book, The Book of Neutronics,' is the culmination of over 50 years studying the martial arts, all martial arts. It is a compilation of five previously published books: The Neuronic Viewpoint, Prologue, The 24 Principles, Neutronics, Outside the Tube. It is recommended that the reader be a martial artist, or study martial arts while reading this book. One who reads without doing is a 'paper tiger,' and that is to be avoided.

This is not a book of forms/techniques.

RESOURCES

Books are available on the internet
Videos are available at MonsterMartialArts.com.

VIDEO COURSES

Matrix Karate ~ the one that started it all. Has a complete art including forms and techniques. Shows how to matrix any art. Includes a book.

Matrix Kung Fu (Monkey Boxing) ~ Matrixes grab arts. Condenses an amazing number of techniques into the forty essential ones which are the root of all. Includes a book.

Matrix Aikido ~ An 80 minute seminar in which I teach several people how to do Aikido. Includes a booklet.

The Master Instructor Course ~ Reveals the six secrets by which ALL martial arts techniques can be made to work. Includes the seven points which make absolutely perfect form. Includes a book.

Shaolin Butterfly ~ Kung Fu condensed into six concepts. Complete with forms and techniques. Includes book.

Butterfly Pa Kua Chang ~ Three methods of Pa Kua Chang. A siple matrixed analysis (Ten hands), a flowing method (teacup) and a more traditional study (Eight Animals). Includes a book.

Matrix Tai Chi Chuan ~ Tai Chi Chuan broken down into core concepts. Extremely workable.

Five Army Tai Chi Chuan ~ Tai Chi made workable through the analysis of the 'five armies.'

Create Your Own Art ~ The only course of its kind, Create/Art shows how to break arts down to concepts, and how to reassemble concepts to create new arts.

Blinding Steel (Monkey Boxing) ~ a complete system of weapons, from empty hands to weapons to disarms.

Matrix Kenjutsu ~ The art of Kenjutsu broken down by matrixing into a simple to learn system.

BOOKS

Matrix Karate ~ This is the grandaddy of my work. It has the beginning concepts, shows how to matrix, and details a complete system of karate. There is a book/video for this course.

Pan Gai Noon ~ is the first book of the Encyclopedia of Karate. It details forms and techniques of the Pan Gai Noon (half hard/half soft) system of Karate. This system provides direct routes back to China, and eventually to the Shaolin Temple.

Kang Duk Won ~ Kang Duk Won is the second book of the Encyclopedia of Karate. It details the forms and techniques of one of the purest systems of karate. There are only a couple. of links between this system and the actual founders of karate.

Kwon Bup ~ An American system of karate. Very linear, very powerful. The founder was able to thrust his finger through a board and leave a hole.

Outlaw Karate ~ One of my first efforts at taking apart and putting together a system of the martial arts. This is a combination of Kang Duk Won and Kwon Bup. It is a system void of posers and possessed of extreme linear power.

Buddha Crane ~ The last system I devised before writing about matrixing. It is quite logical, shows how to take apart systems and put them together.

Matrix Karate Series ~ Five books, white, green, brown, black and master, which demonstrate, in detail the workings of matrixing.

The Book of Five Arts ~ A very concise but meaty book outlining five, specific and matrixed arts. It shows the three House forms of Matrix Karate, four butterfly forms from Shaolin Butterfly kung fu, eight teacup forms from Pa Kua Chang, the nine squares from Matrix Tai Chi Chuan, and the essence of Monkey Boxing.

Chiang Nan: How to Translate Karate into Tai Chi Chuan ~ A book demonstrating how a pure form of karate can be altered without losing the essence. Indeed, in this case any alteration tends to make the art more powerful.

The Last Martial Arts Book: Nine Square Diagram Boxing ~ A method that condenses all of the martial arts into nine techniques, which techniques are then put on a foot pattern, and explored for an amazing number of techniques.

The Book of Matrixing ~ combines several smaller books on the subject of matrixing which I have written over the years. A very thorough and in depth look at the logic behind matrixing.

The Book of Neutronics ~ combines several smaller books on the subject of neutronics which I have written over the years. A very thorough and in depth look at the science/philosophy of Neutronics.

For a more complete list go to MonsterMartialArts.com.

Novels

One of the things I love to do in my spare time is write novels. Many of my novels incorporate martial arts.

The Monkeyland Series (six books)
From madmen to aliens, you will find out who is running planet earth!

The Machina Series (three books)

A terrorist detonates an atomic bomb in Los Angeles, that causes an earthquake, 'The Big One,' then something really bad happens.

The Wizard of Parts (three books)

To be a wizard one must go insane, kill himself, and discover the secret of the universe.

Yancy (three books)

A young cowboy decides to become a gunfighter.